Asparagus
and other friends

Asparagus
and other friends

Sixty Relief Engravings of Flowers, Fruits and Vegetables

TREVOR HADDRELL

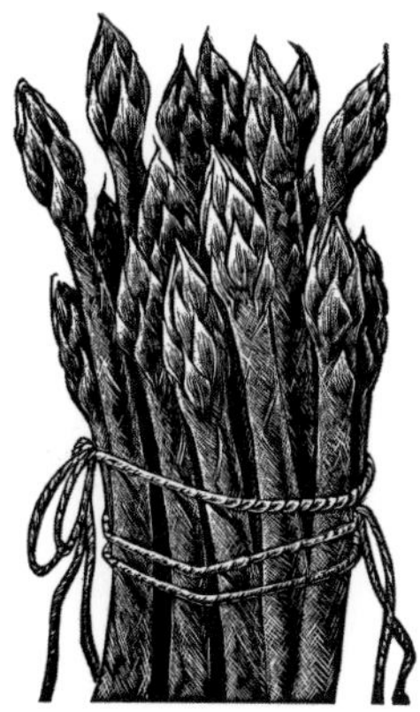

redcliffe

First published in 2005 by Redcliffe Press Ltd.,
81g Pembroke Road, Bristol BS8 3EA

0117 929 8363

ISBN 1 904537 37 5

British Library Cataloguing-in-Publication Data
A catalogue record for this book is available from
the British Library

Design and typesetting by Stephen Morris Communications,
smc@freeuk.com Bristol and Liverpool
Printed and bound in Malta by Gutenberg Press Ltd

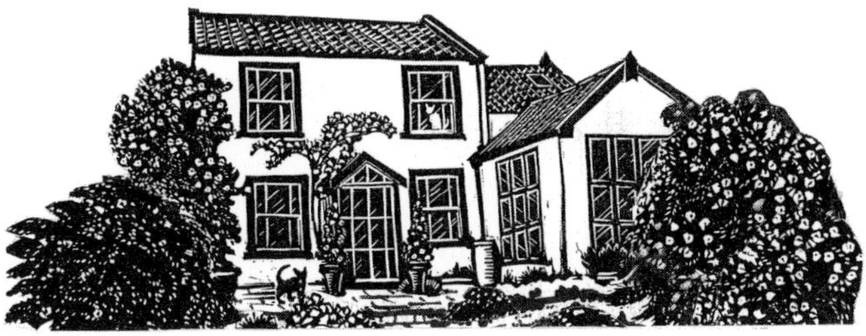

Introduction

The reproductions in this volume come from an ever-expanding series of engravings of natural forms which I began over ten years ago, when I first started to explore this method of relief print-making.

I have been fortunate to have a talented and obsessive gardener as my partner for almost thirty years, now, and as a result, we have a fascinating garden around our home, containing a wide variety of flowering plants, shrubs and trees, a vegetable patch and an allotment nearby. These provide me with an endless supply of interesting subjects the whole year round.

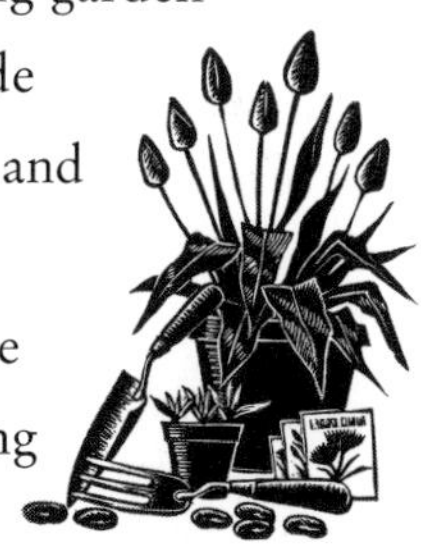

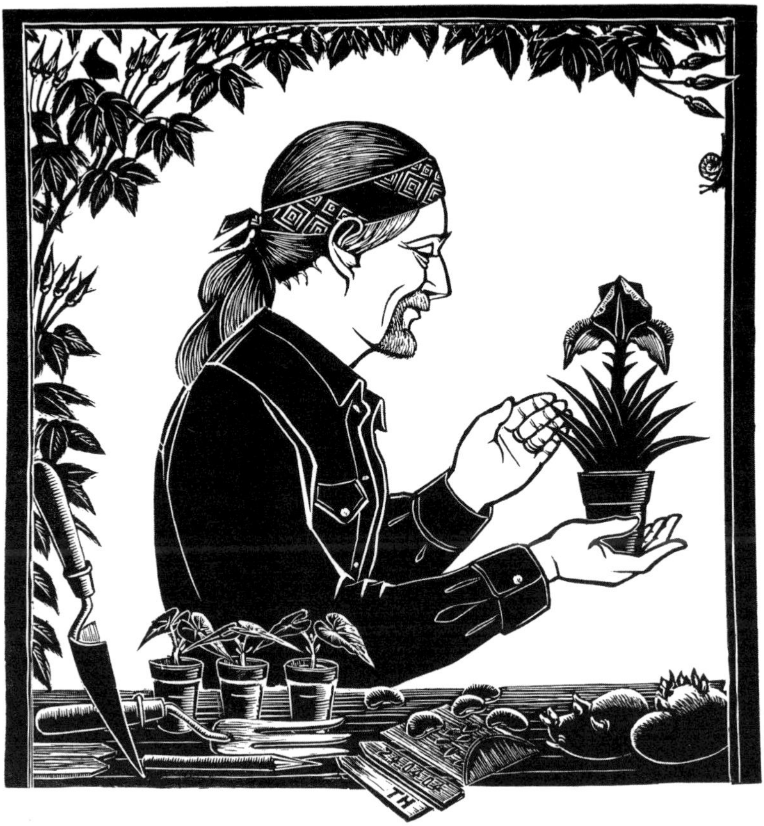

The Gardener:

John, whose green fingers are responsible for producing most of the subjects illustrated in this volume.

Contents

The Technique

In these designs, I have been particularly influenced by the monumental studies of natural forms by the early photographer, Karl Blossfeldt, by the powerful wood-engravings of artists such as Eric Ravilious, Clare Leighton and Gertrude Hermes, and also the work of the Japanese wood-block artists such as Hokusai and Hiroshige. Their work fills me with admiration and provides me with much stimulus and inspiration.

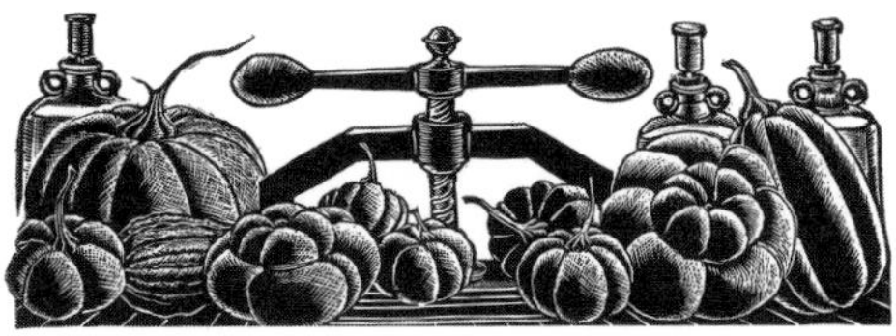

I begin my work by making sketches from direct observation of several examples of the particular subject which has appealed to me (see pages from my sketchbook reproduced here on pages 10 and 11). The aim is not only to come to an understanding of the individual form in front of me but also to try to work out a way of suggesting how that form will develop and change with the passage of time. Sometimes, this can be done by drawing the same specimen over a number of days and then combining studies in the final design (e.g. ***Runner Bean Sprouts*** plate 4).

At other times, the aim is to try to imply this development by refining down the many studies of different specimens into a design of just a few forms which demonstrate what I've come to feel are the 'archetypal' features of the subject (e.g. the studies of ***Five Florence Fennel*** plate 6).

I rarely turn a sketch from observation into an engraving simply by copying line for line what is in my sketchbook. There is usually much careful further 'choreographing' of the linear and tonal rhythms to be done to the initial sketch before it yields the possibility of becoming a workable engraving.

These designs are intended to be, first and foremost, effective

Two pages from my sketchbook

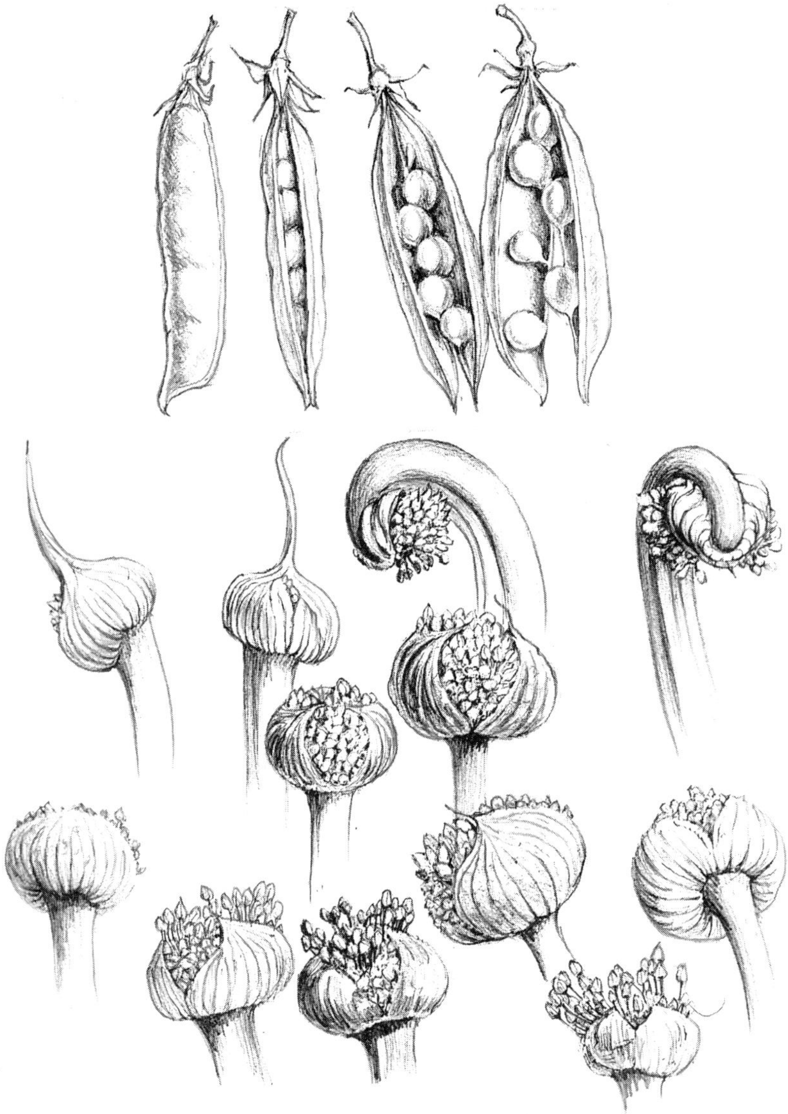

Pencil drawings from observation:
Peas and Onion Seedheads (used for reference in plates 24 and 10).

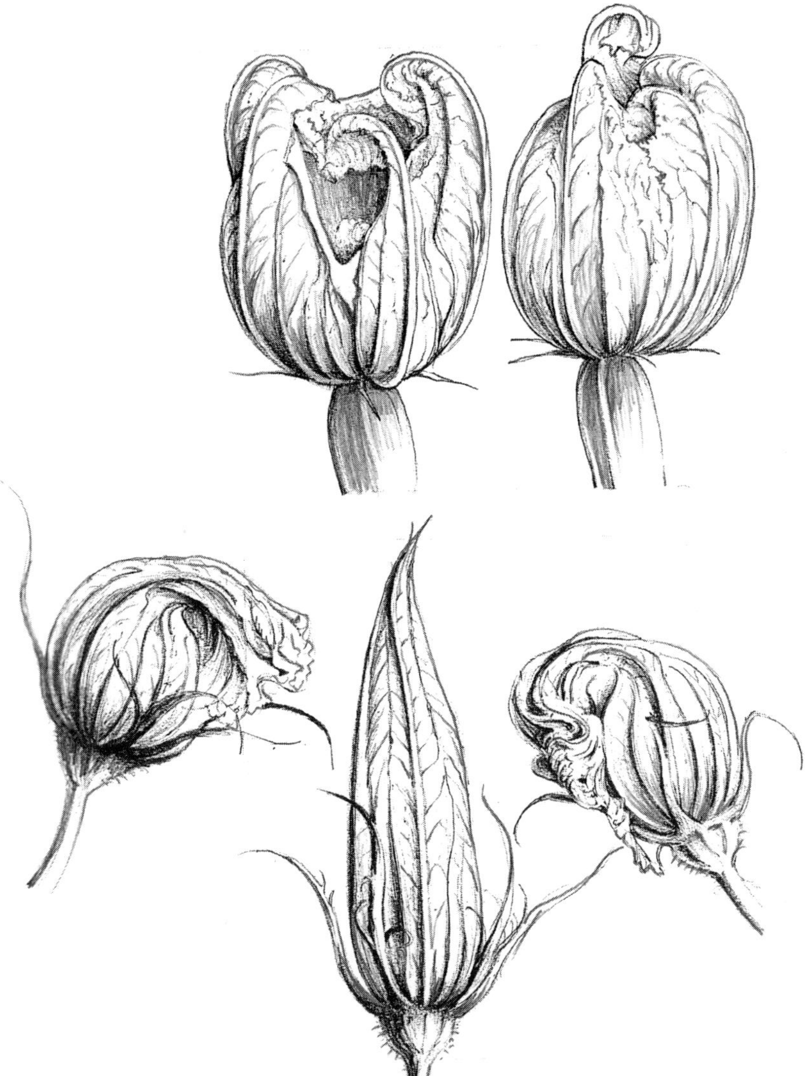

Pencil drawings from observation:
Courgette Flowers (used in plates 11 and 12).

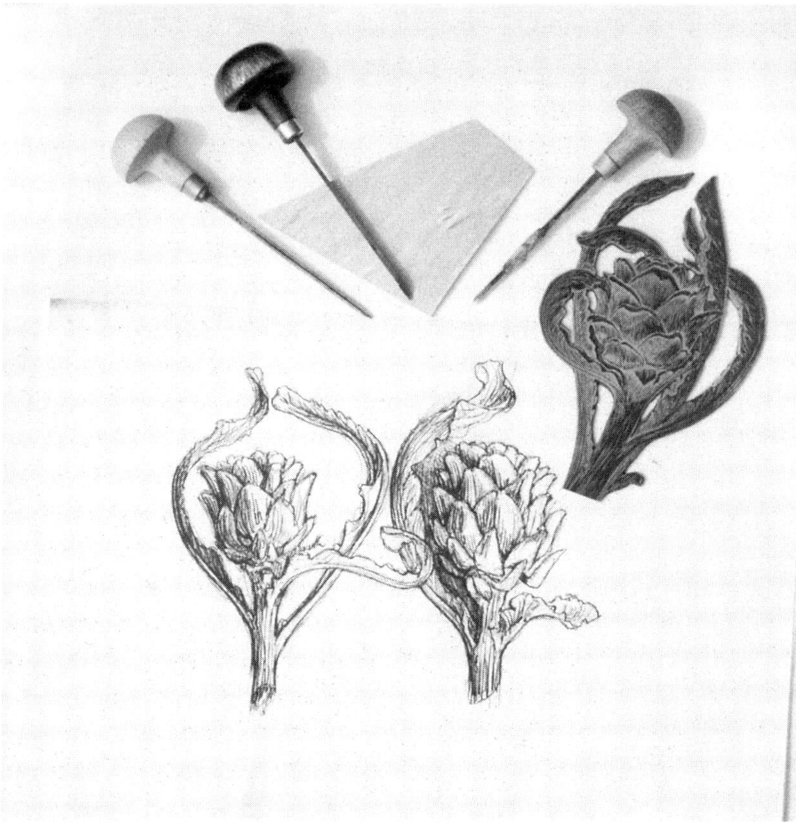

This photograph shows a fragment of the type of vinyl I use with a few engraved cuts in its surface and also some of the tools I use. To the right of the drawings of the artichokes in my sketchbook is the actual engraved block used to make the design reproduced in this volume (plate 18).

abstract designs in the language of black and white engraving, rather than pedantic botanical studies of the subjects.

Once I am satisfied I have developed the sketch sufficiently, I then trace it and transfer it, reversed, onto a vinyl block, ready for engraving. This is heavy-duty flooring vinyl, as used in schools and offices, about 1mm thick. (I first came to experiment with this as a surface for engraving when a new floor was laid in the art studio of the school where I taught and all the off-cuts were 'donated' to us by the workmen.)

I prefer to use a medium-grey coloured vinyl – the transferred pencil line is easy to see on this and it is then simple to go over it with a waterproof black felt-tip pen. Engraved marks on this vinyl appear lighter in colour than the original surface so the progress of the design can be easily monitored.

The tools I use for engraving are a mixture of fine lino-cutting gouges and traditional wood-engraving tools.

These are relief prints, i.e. whatever is cut out of the surface of the block will read as an area of white in the final print, whatever is left untouched will appear black.

Tonal variations (shading) can be suggested by fine stipplings or hatchings produced with differently shaped tools.

Initially, it may seem odd to be working in reverse like this – adding the light areas, rather than darks ones as one usually does when drawing. I found it became easier, though, when I thought of it as drawing in white on a black surface. The brain appears to adjust quite quickly to working in reverse. I hardly seem to notice I'm doing it, these days.

When the block is fully engraved, ink is carefully rolled onto the surface, a piece of paper is placed on top, a soft blanket on top of this and then the whole ensemble is passed through a roller press to produce the impression.

Limited Edition Prints

For the individually handmade original prints, which I produce directly from the engraved blocks, I use a heavyweight, fine art paper called Somerset Satin. It is made in Wookey, near Wells, is 100% acid free and of conservation standard.
These prints have a pleasing, slightly embossed appearance when they come off the press: much more sensuous than a photographic reproduction.

Each print is signed and numbered and editions are limited as indicated.

Several of these engravings have been selected for the annual exhibitions of the Royal West of England Academy in Bristol and also for the annual touring exhibitions of the Society of Wood Engravers.

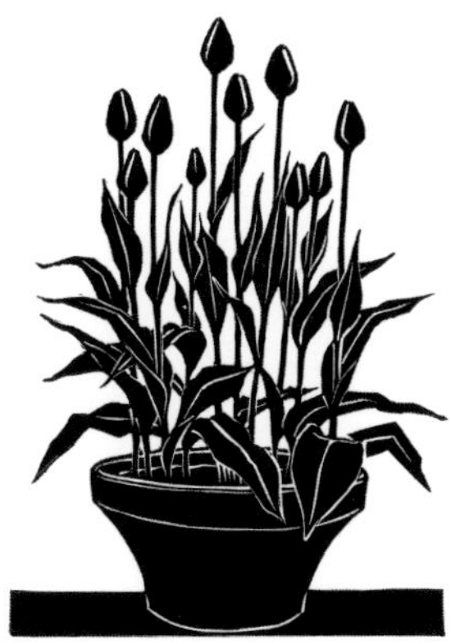

List of Plates

(All works are reproduced actual size except where otherwise indicated)

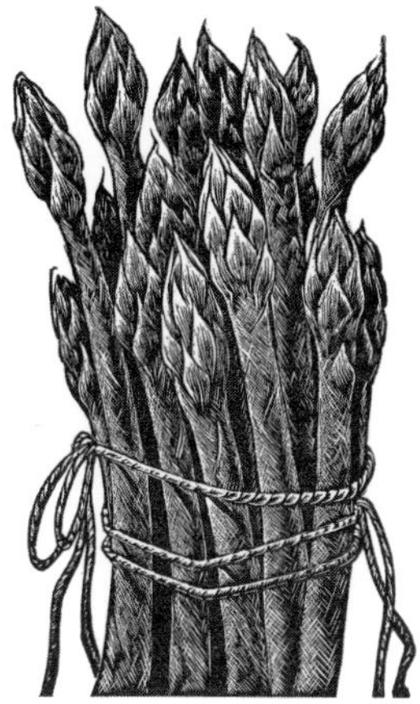

From the Allotment

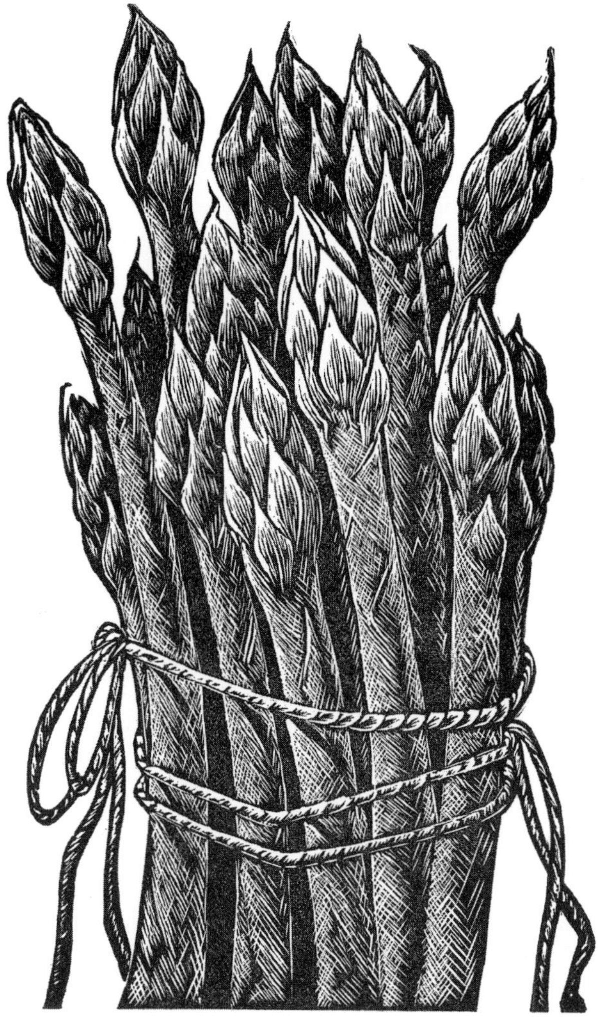

1 Asparagus Spears

This was our entire harvest of asparagus after seven years of effort, so I felt I had to record the precious spears in an engraving before we ate them.

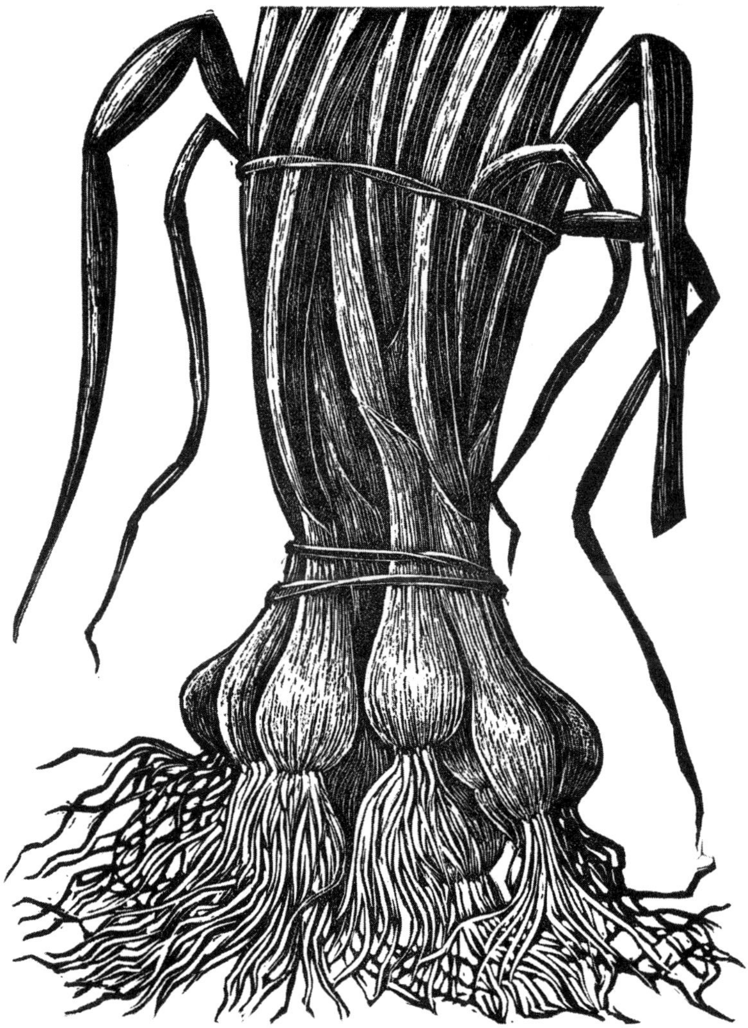

2 Spring Onions

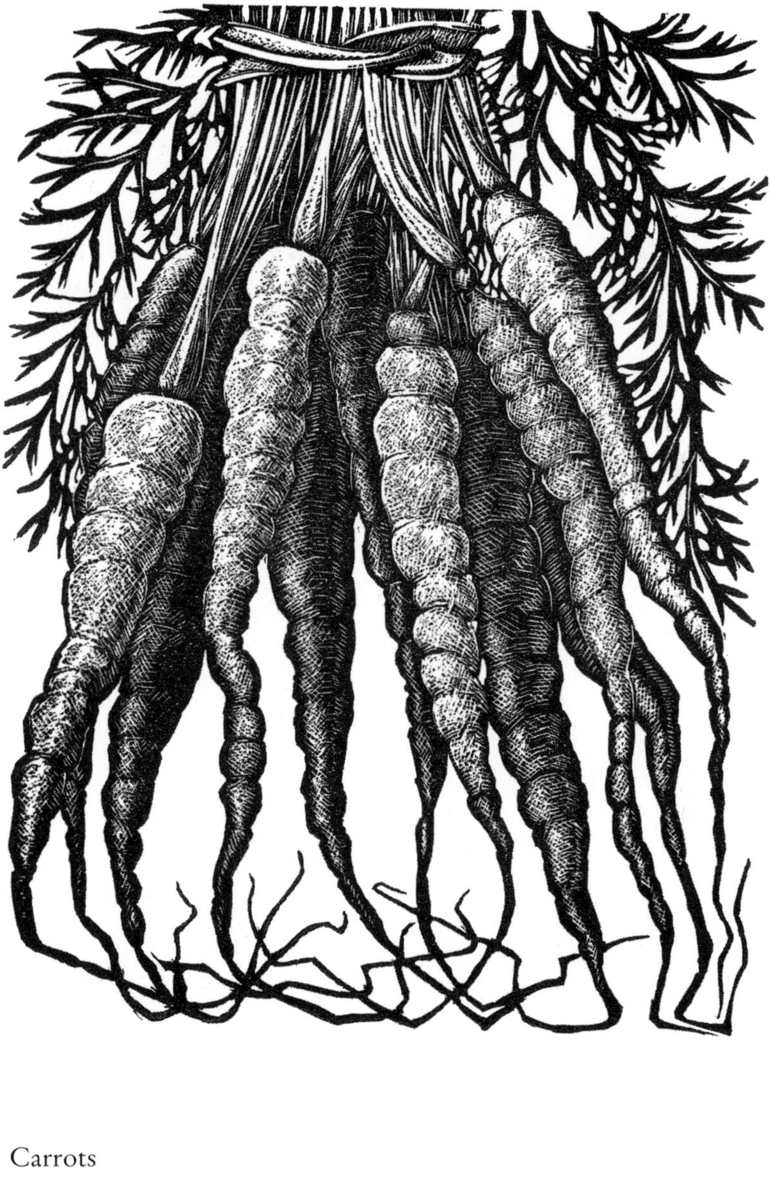

3 Carrots

Picked straight from the allotment. I wish it was possible to convey the distinctive aroma of them as well as their visual appearance.

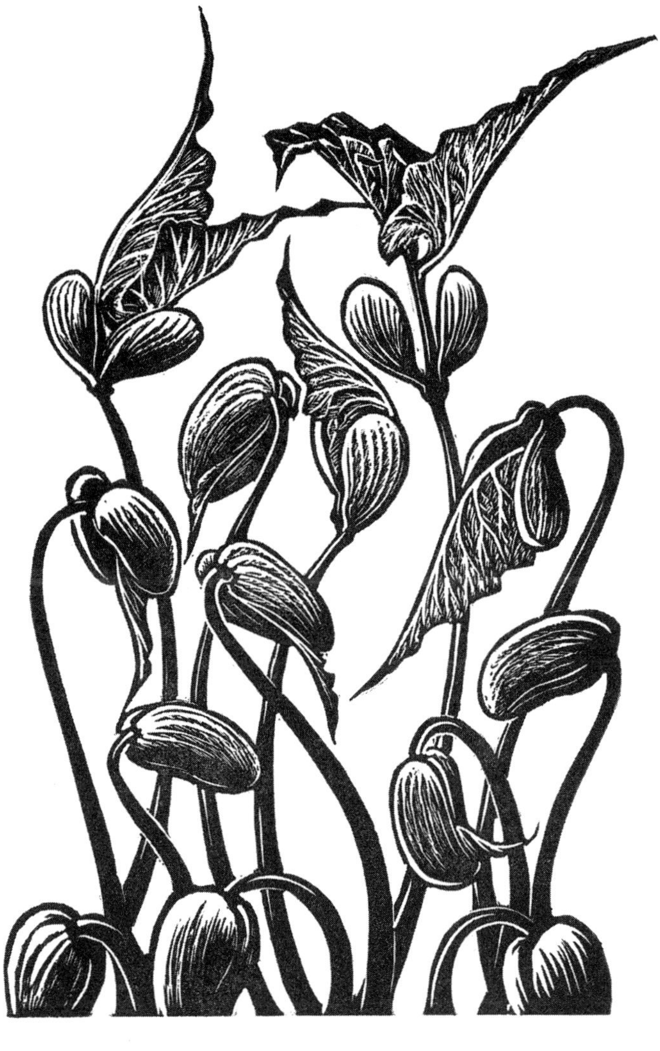

4 Runner Bean Sprouts

This is the same runner bean sketched each day for about a fortnight. I was aiming for a composition which expressed the whole growth pattern of the young plant.

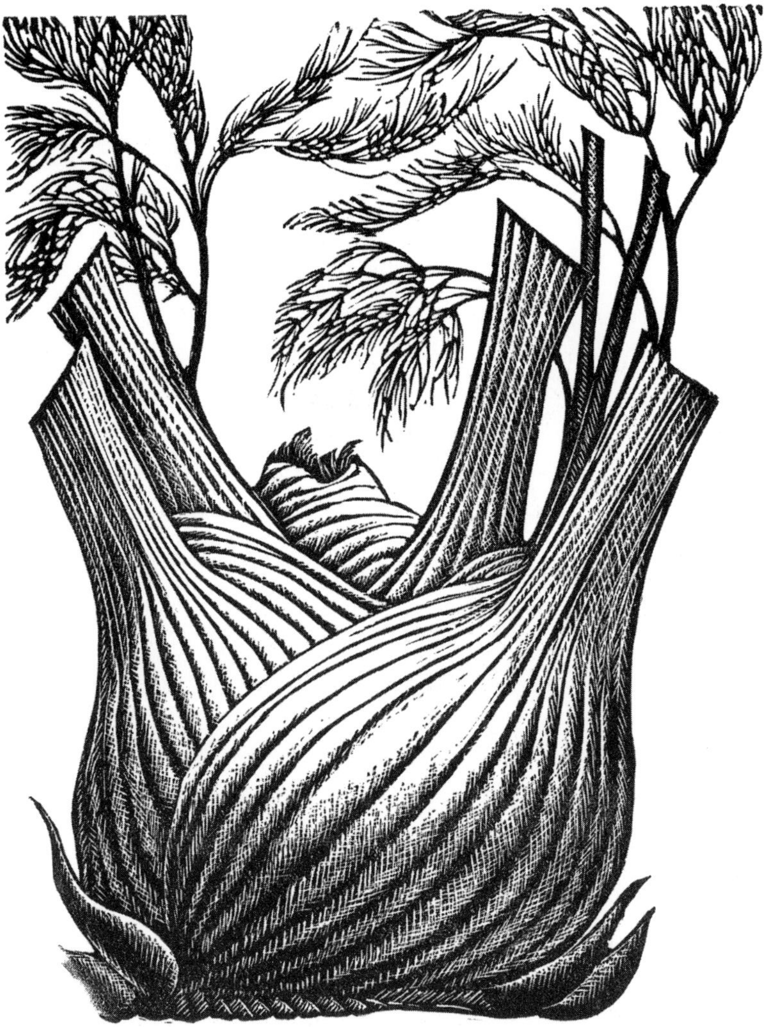

5 Fennel

The linear furrows on the surface of these bulbs and the feathery foliage reminded me of a landscape with ploughed fields.

We've never had much success in attempting to grow fennel bulbs – unlike *La Nonna* of a family I knew in the Veneto who told me: *You just throw the seeds on the ground, water well, then, a few weeks later, you pick them – no problem!* It certainly worked for her.

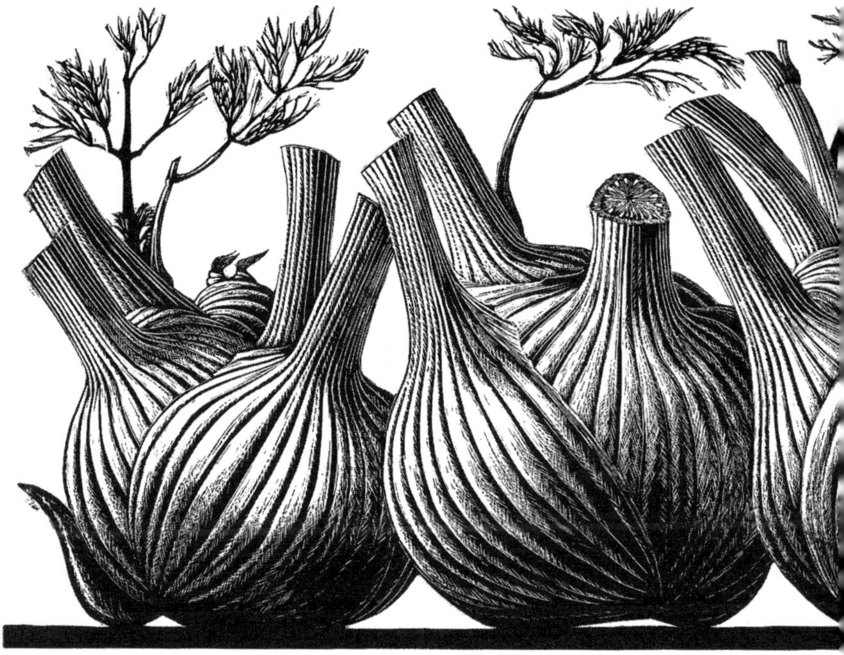

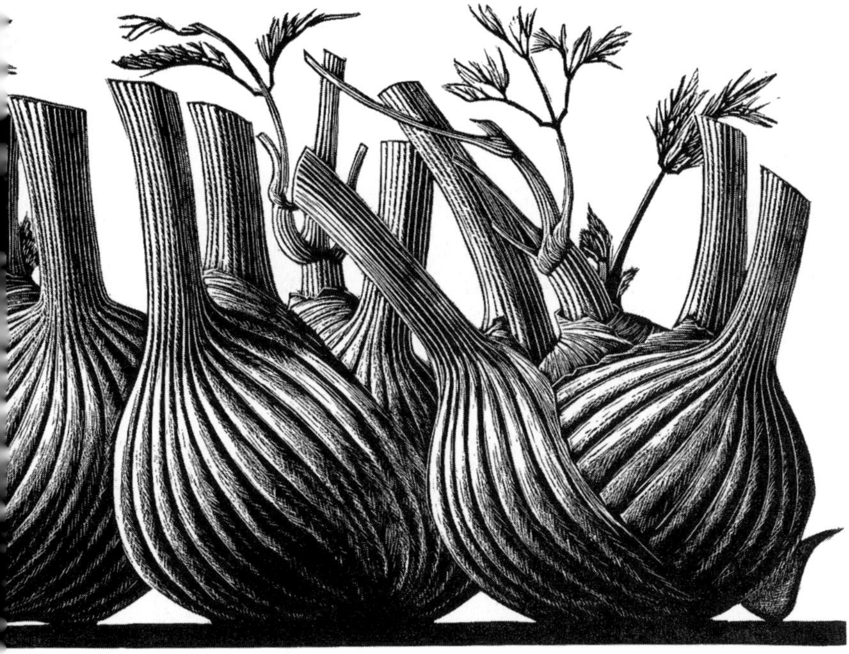

6 Five Florence Fennel

I wanted to make a tight, formal composition from these five bulbs (actually, three, drawn from different angles) and, at the same time, to develop the suggestion that they could also be read as a ploughed landscape.

(Reduced from 170mm x 480mm, 7 x 18 1/2 inches)

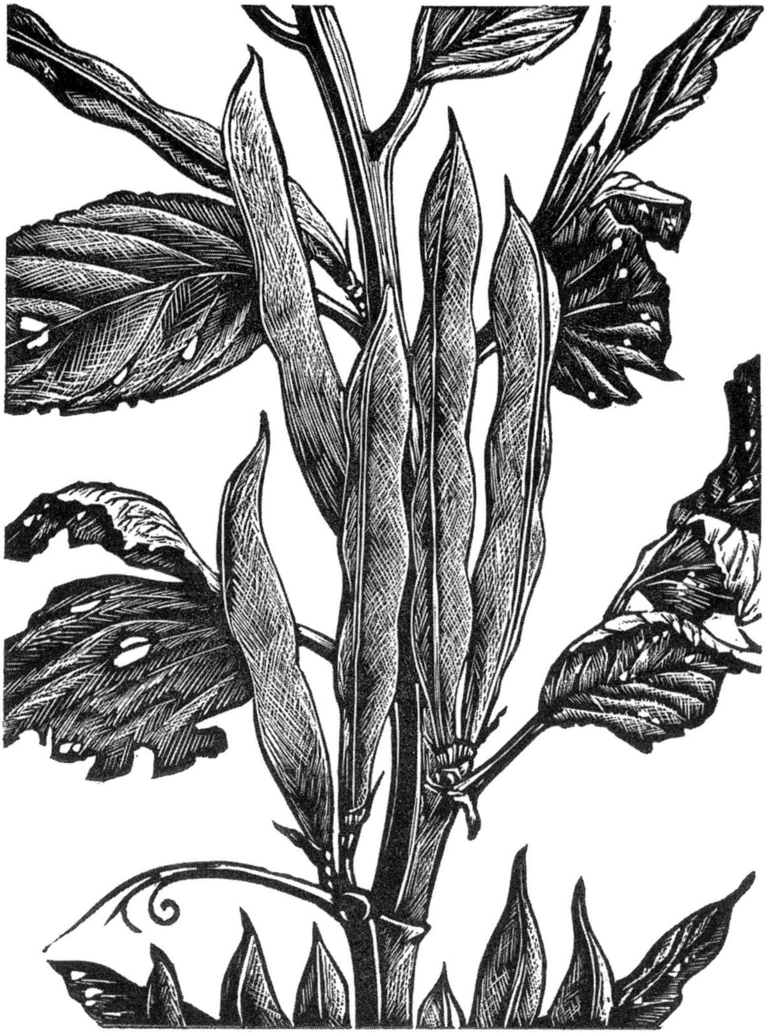

7 Broad Beans

Many people think this engraving is upside down but these beans really do grow upwards like this.

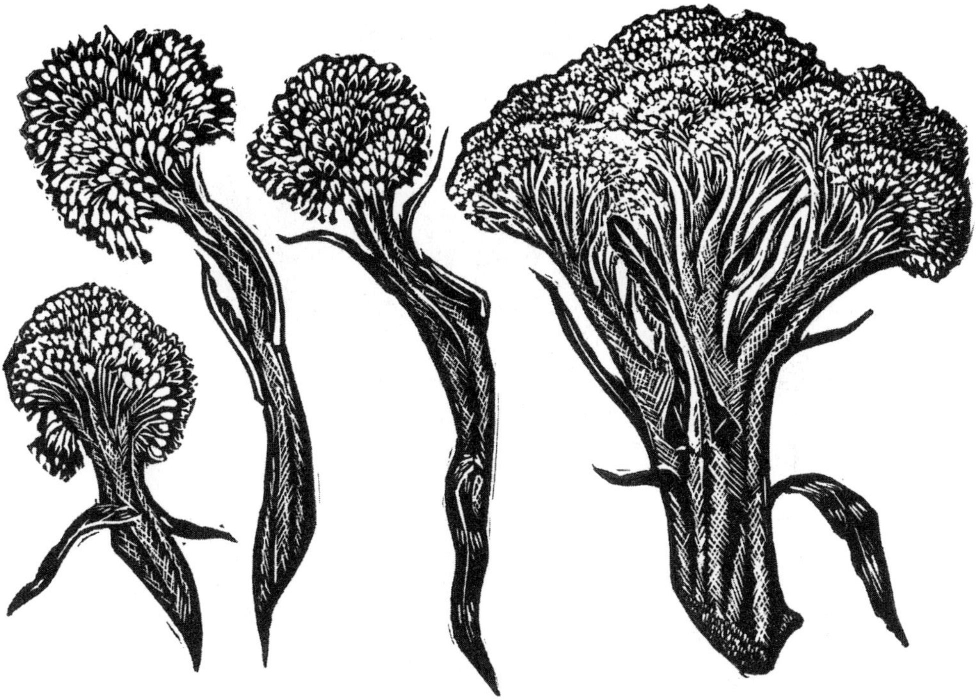

8 Broccoli

This was my first attempt at this subject before the larger version illustrated next.

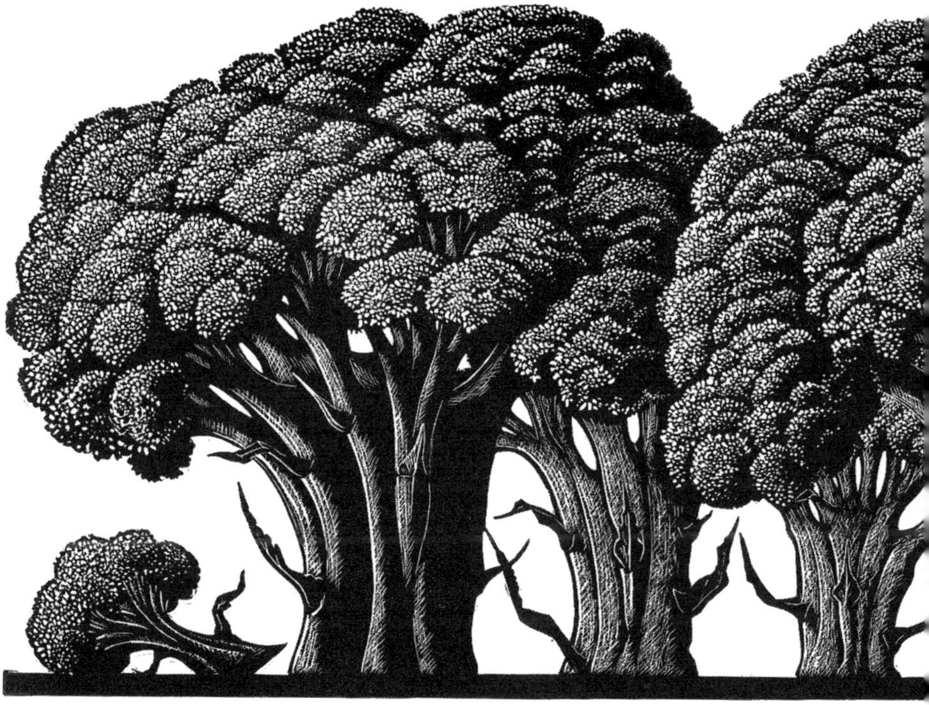

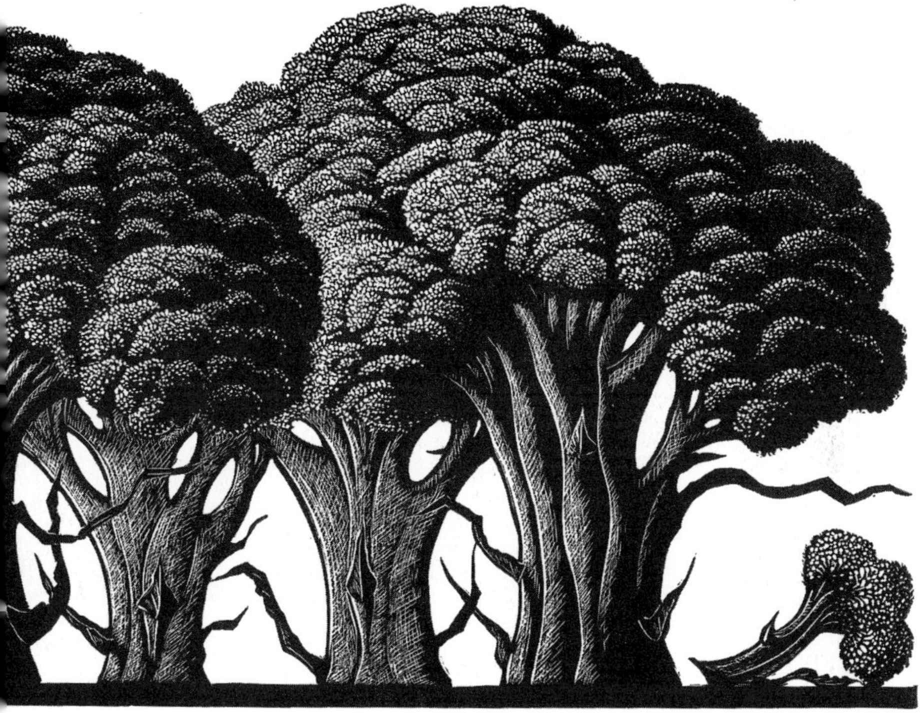

9 Broccoli Forest

I have read of Renaissance artists who used studies of this vegetable to enable them to paint trees in their landscapes. Maintaining an ambiguity of scale was crucial here to keep both interpretations (i.e. trees and broccoli) simultaneously possible.

(Reduced from 170mm x 480mm, 7 x 18 1/2 inches)

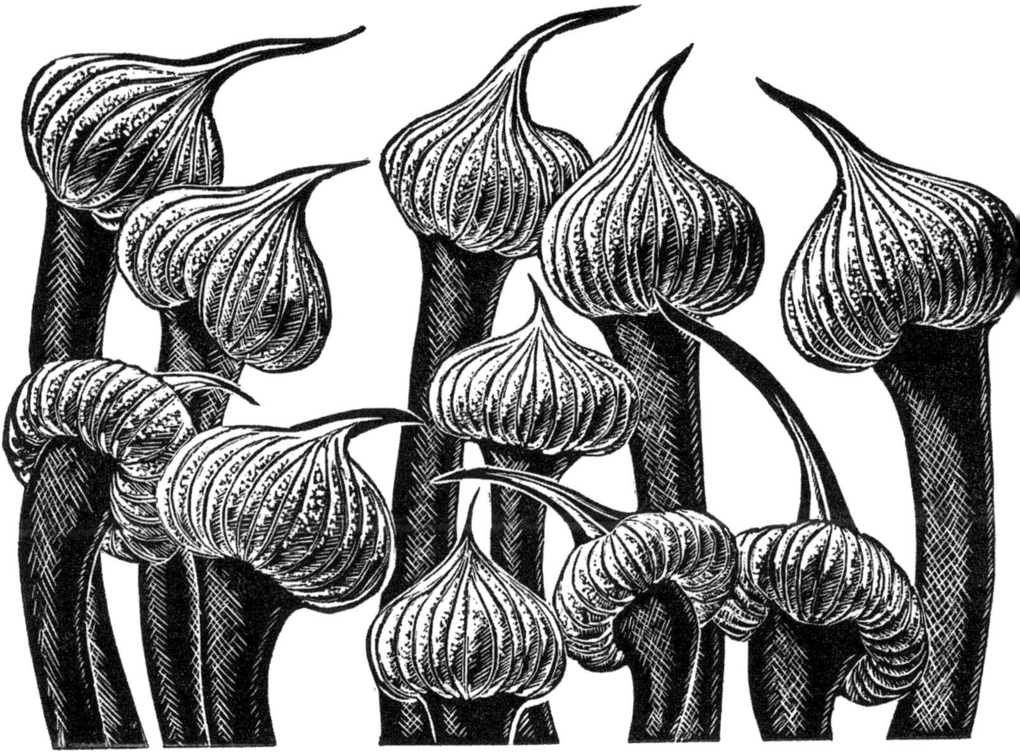

10 Onion Seedheads

One year, all our onions bolted but I spent days sketching the development of the turban-shaped seedheads in my sketchbook and then combined several studies in this engraving.

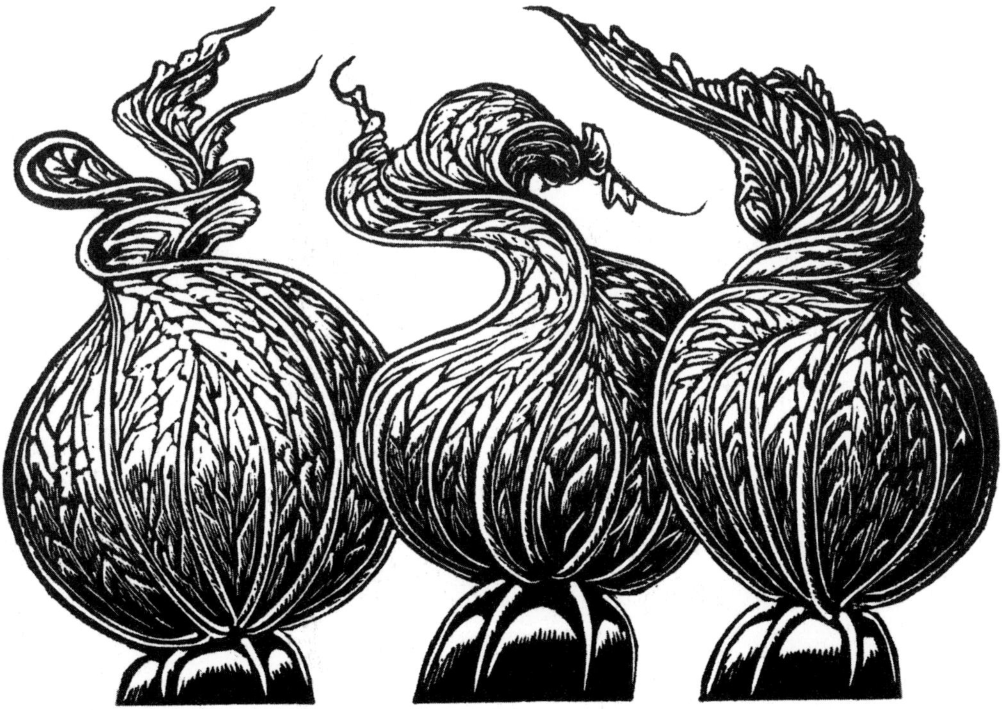

11 Three Courgette Flowers

This was my first attempt at this subject before the larger, more detailed, study of five flowers illustrated next.

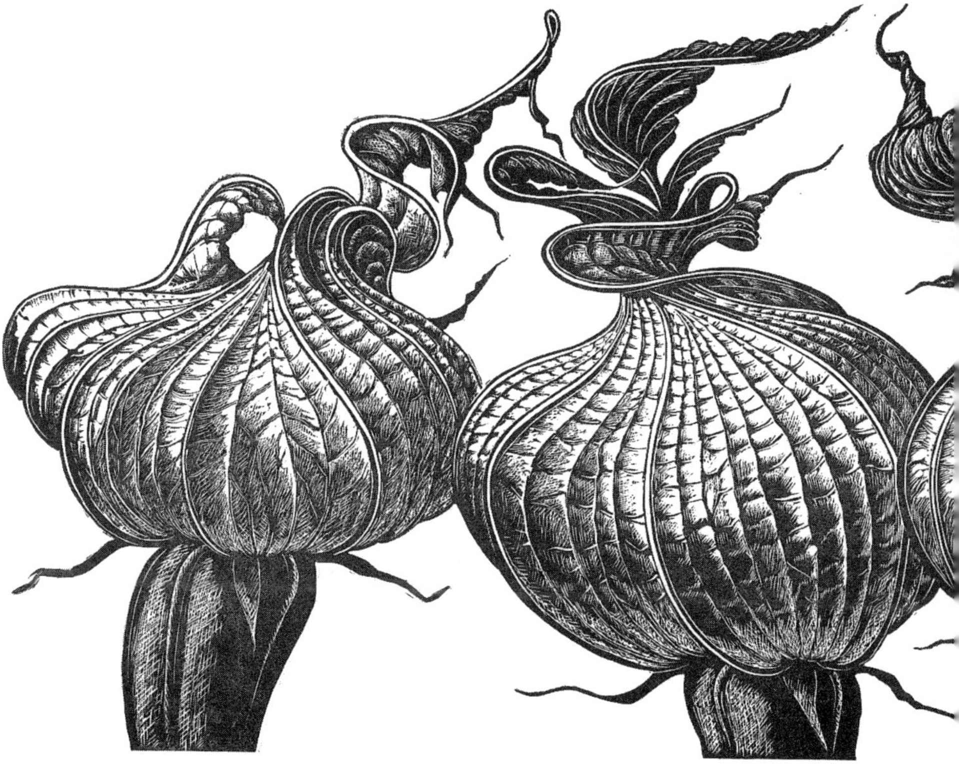

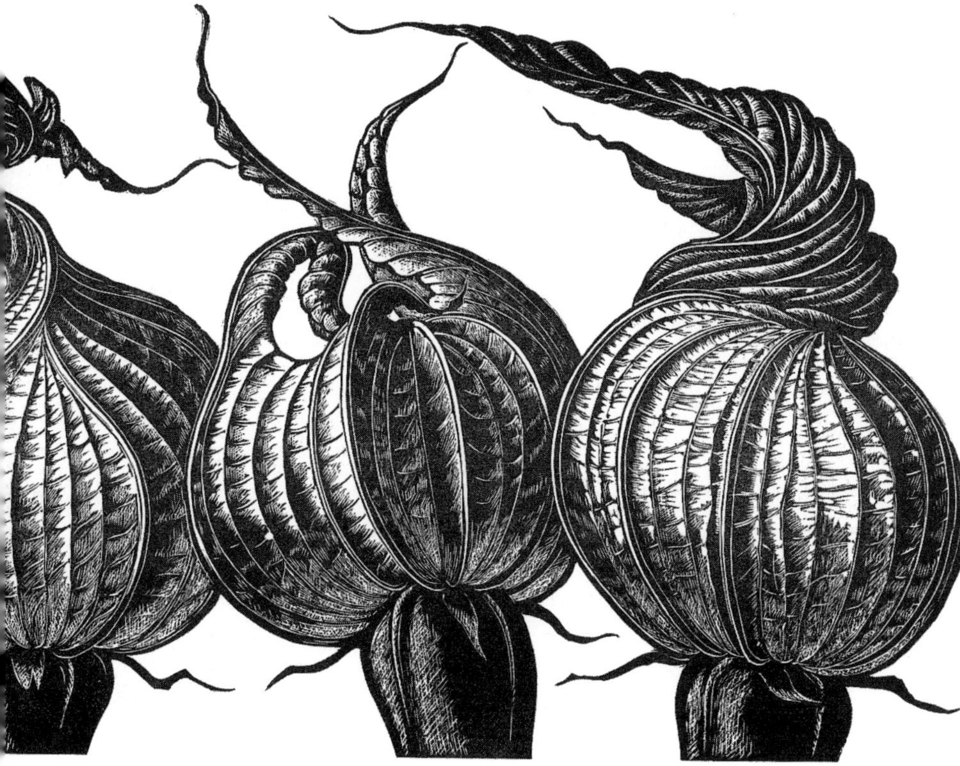

12 Five Courgette Flowers

These were picked from the vegetable patch to eat but I became fascinated by the way the cup-shaped flowers began to collapse within seconds into these weird, dancing forms. Supper was delayed, once again, so I could draw them.

(Reduced from 170mm x 480mm, 7 x 18 1/2 inches)

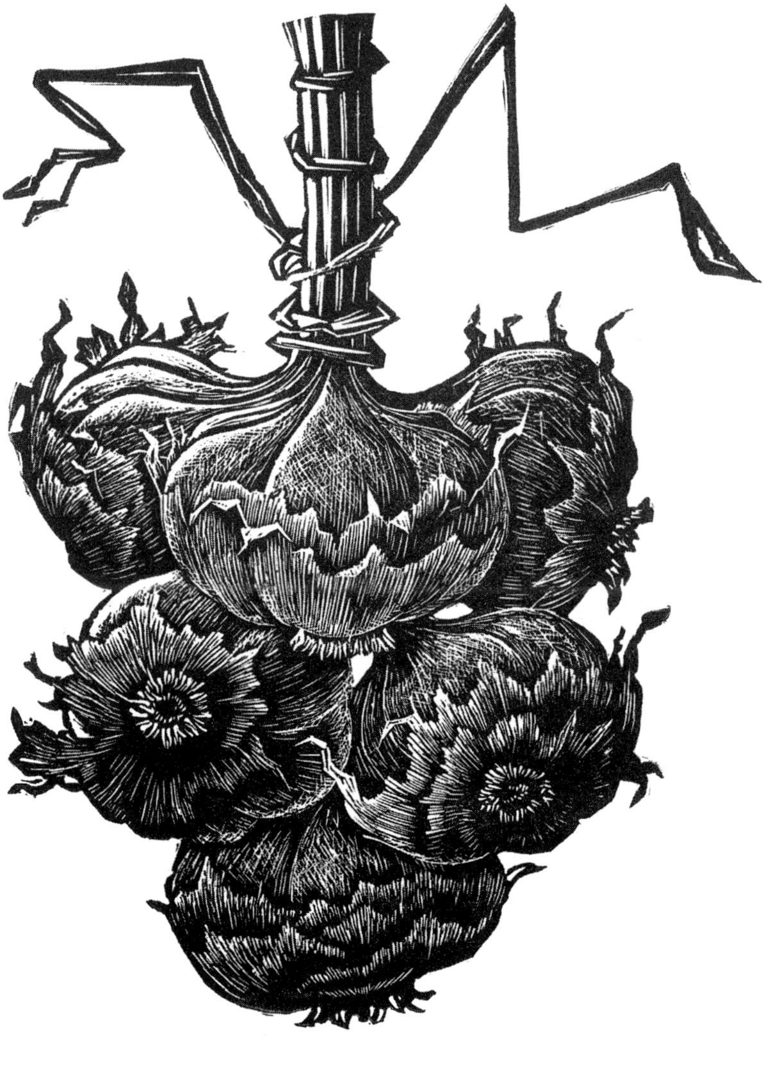

13 Garlic

The aroma of freshly harvested garlic is an annual delight and the tied bunches of bulbs hanging in the kitchen are very tempting to draw. I liked the way the skins began to split and flake on these examples as they dried out.

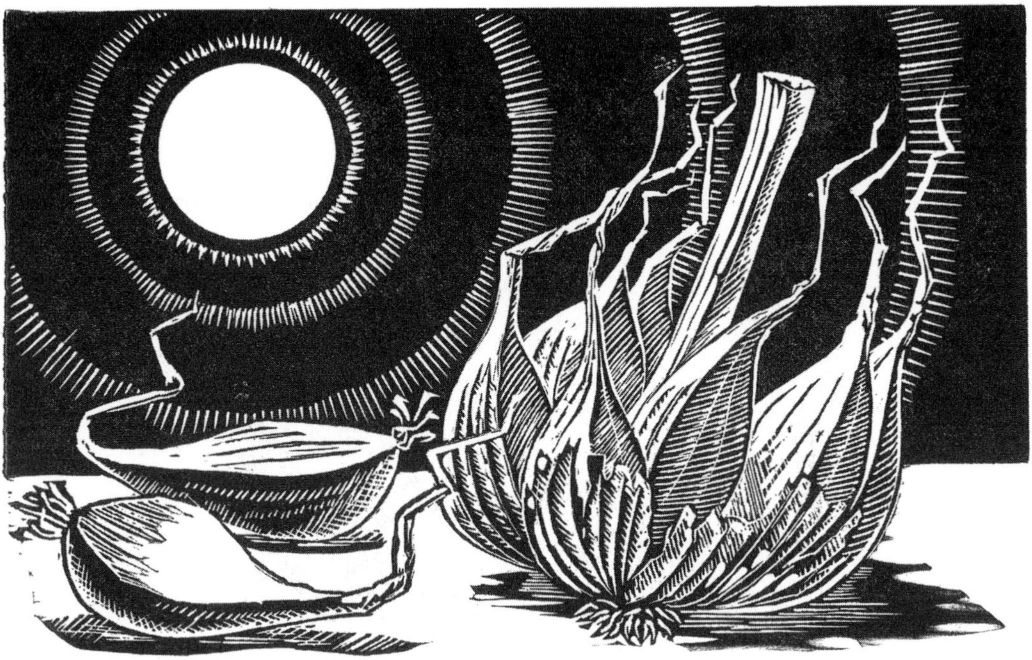

14 Garlic by Moonlight

15 Cardoon

We read that this vegetable was very popular in Victorian times but it has since fallen out of favour in this country.

We discovered why when we tried to eat it! It was incredibly bitter, no matter how we cooked it.

I've seen it often on Italian market stalls so there must be some secret to cooking it which we've not discovered.

It does make an impressive display on the allotment, though, and its purple thistle-like flowers are regularly used dried in floral arrangements.

(Reduced from 370mm x 110mm, 14 1/2 x 4 1/2 inches)

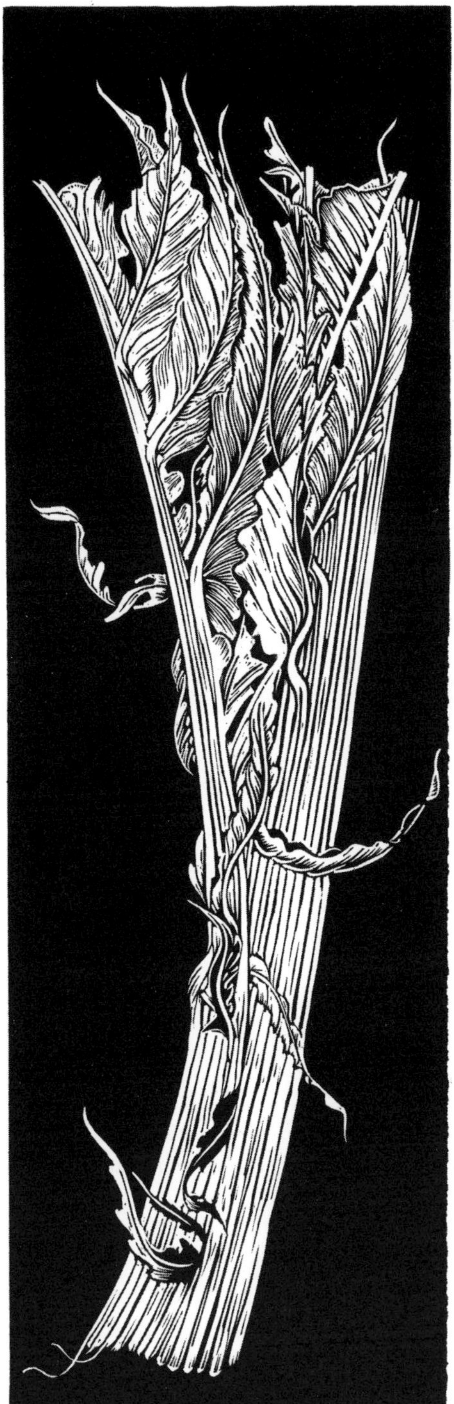

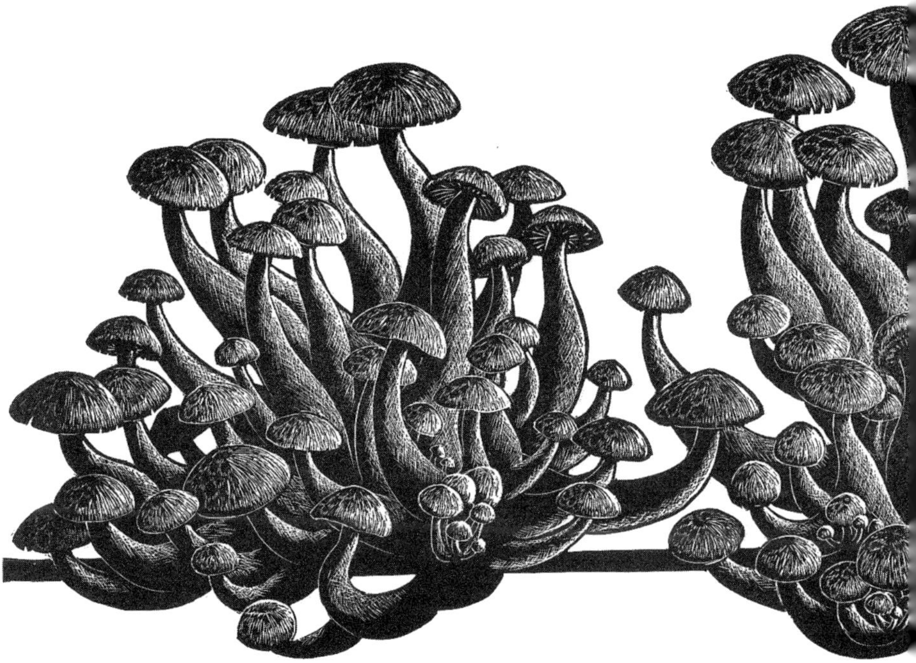

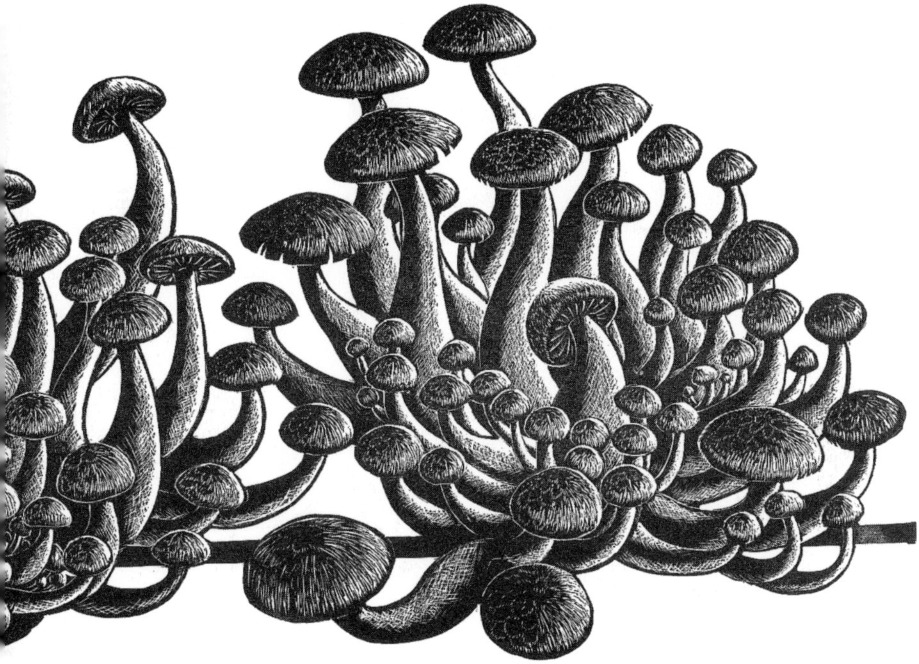

16 Japanese Mushrooms (Shimeji)

I found these in our local organic supermarket and kept them growing on for over a week so I could sketch their development each evening. I liked their alien, slightly menacing, character.

(Reduced from 170mm x 480mm, 7 x 18 1/2 inches)

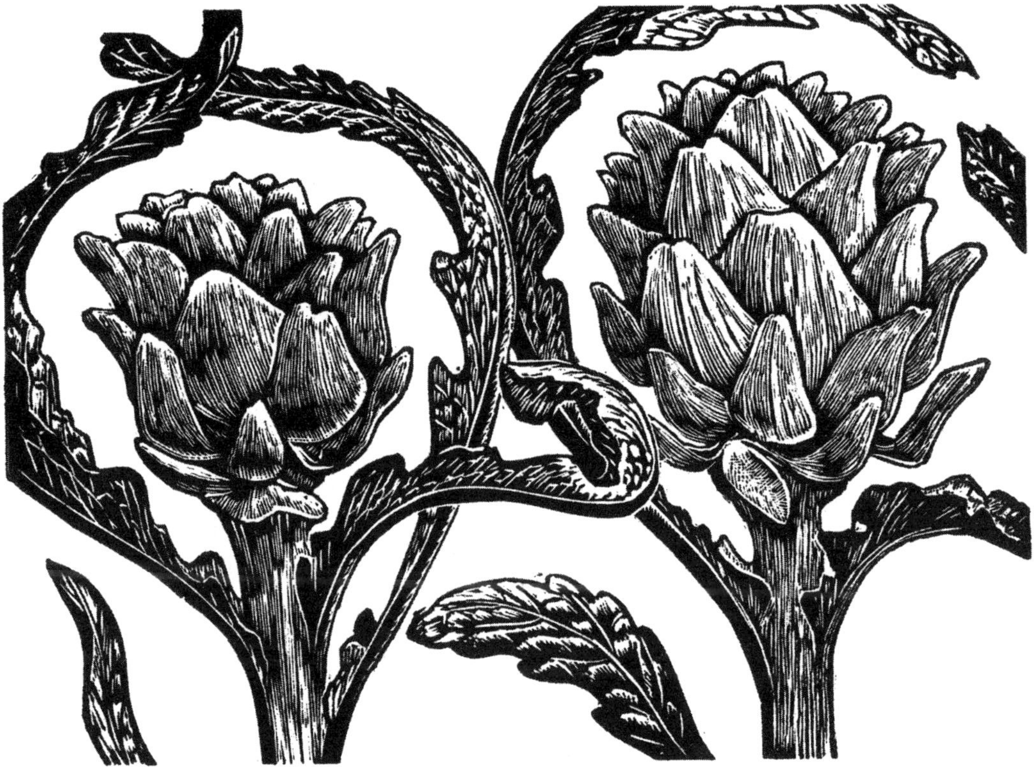

17 Artichokes

This was a first attempt at this subject, drawn after a particularly good crop.

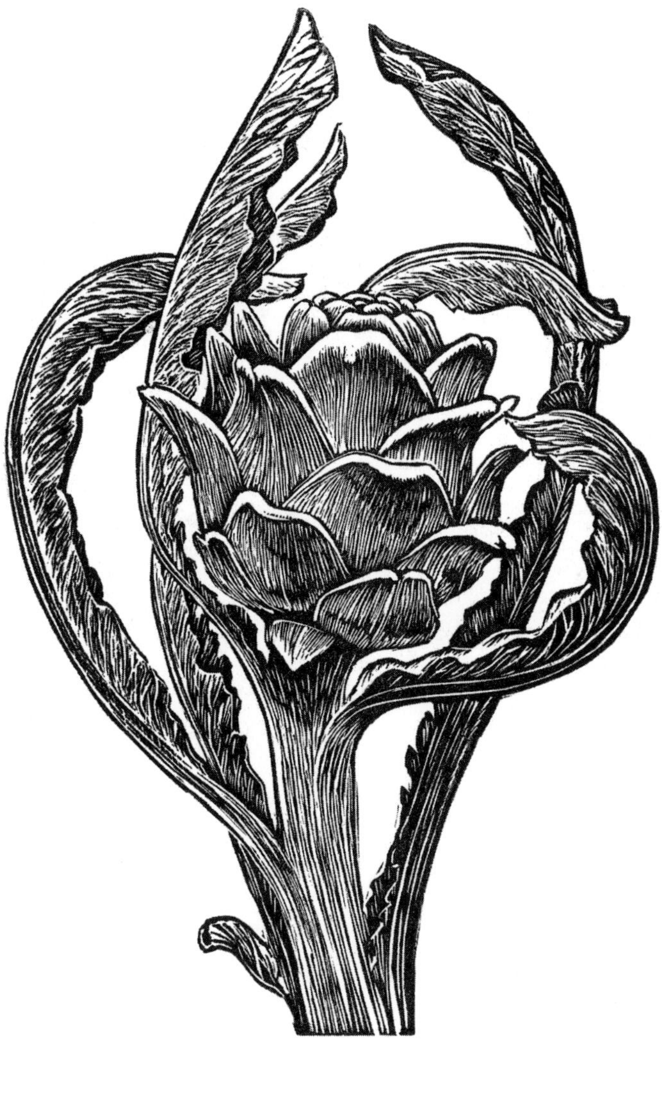

18 Artichoke

This study of a single example was my second attempt which allows the rhythms between the choke and foliage to flow more freely.

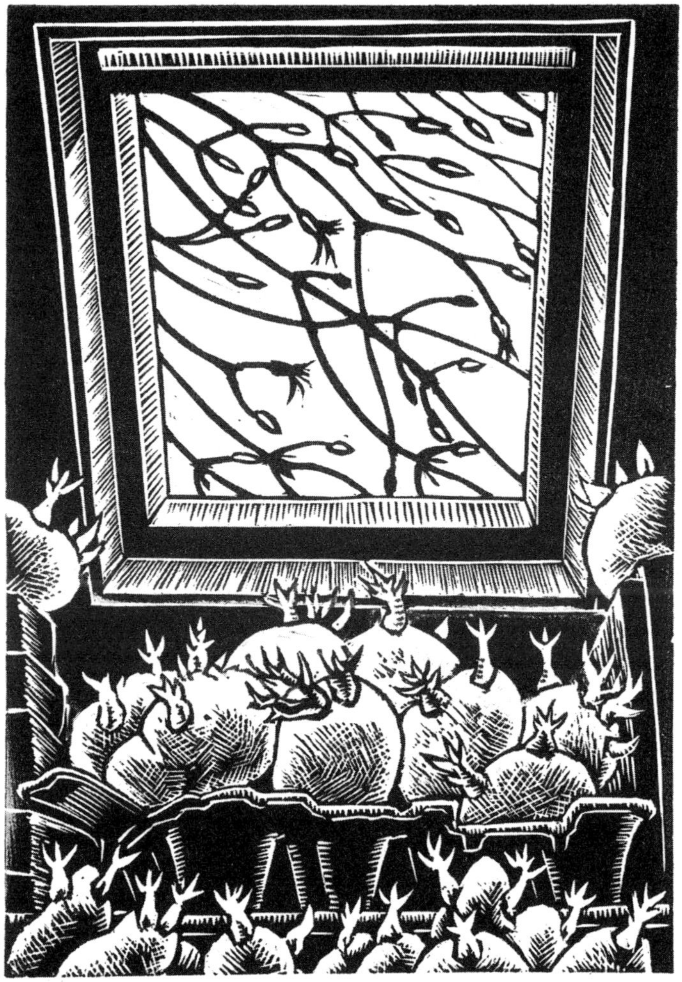

19 Chitting Potatoes

These were in the loft room with overhead daylight to encourage sprouting. Outside, the sycamore buds were also developing.

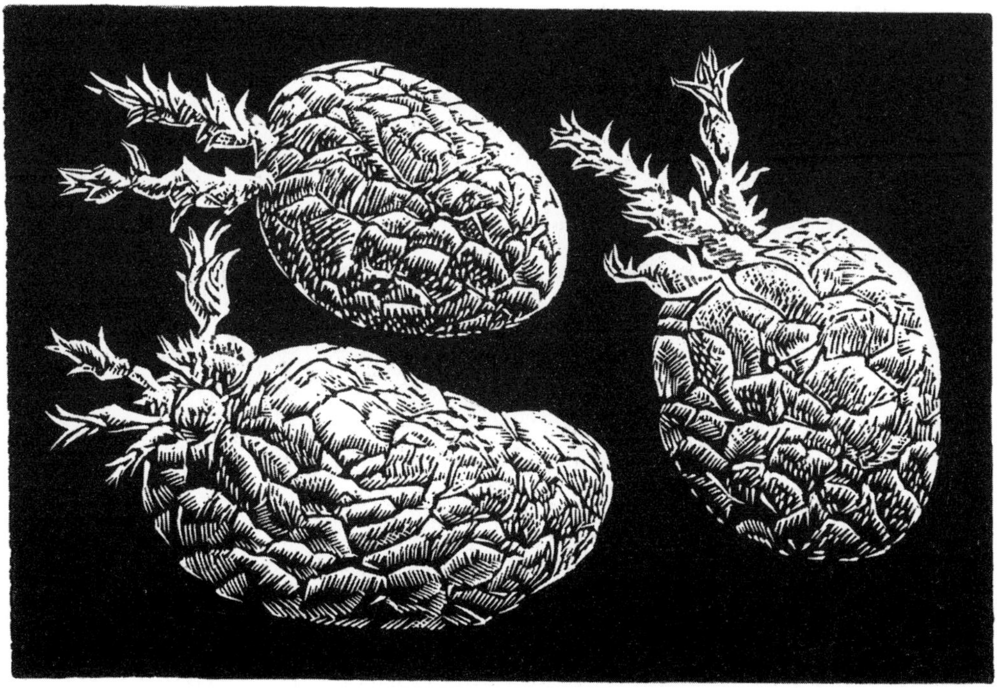

20 Sprouting Potatoes

I found these in a bag in the back of a cupboard at the school where I taught. They were the forgotten remnants of the ones I'd taken in to use for potato prints months earlier. The cracked and cratered surfaces contrasted dramatically with the smooth, translucent shoots and tiny, sparkling green leaves trying to form.

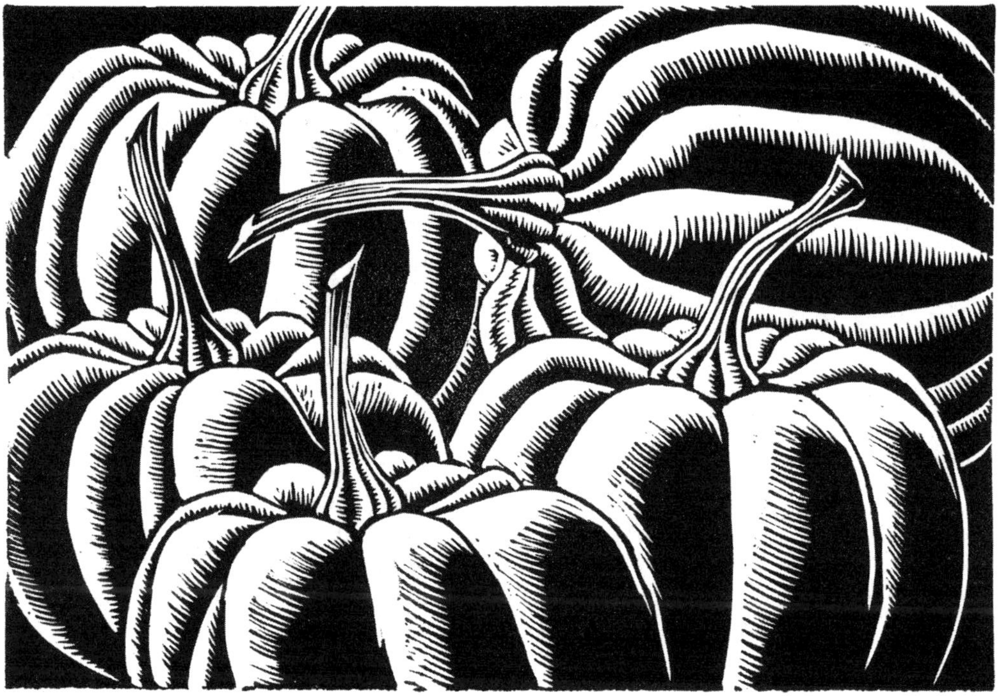

21 Pumpkins

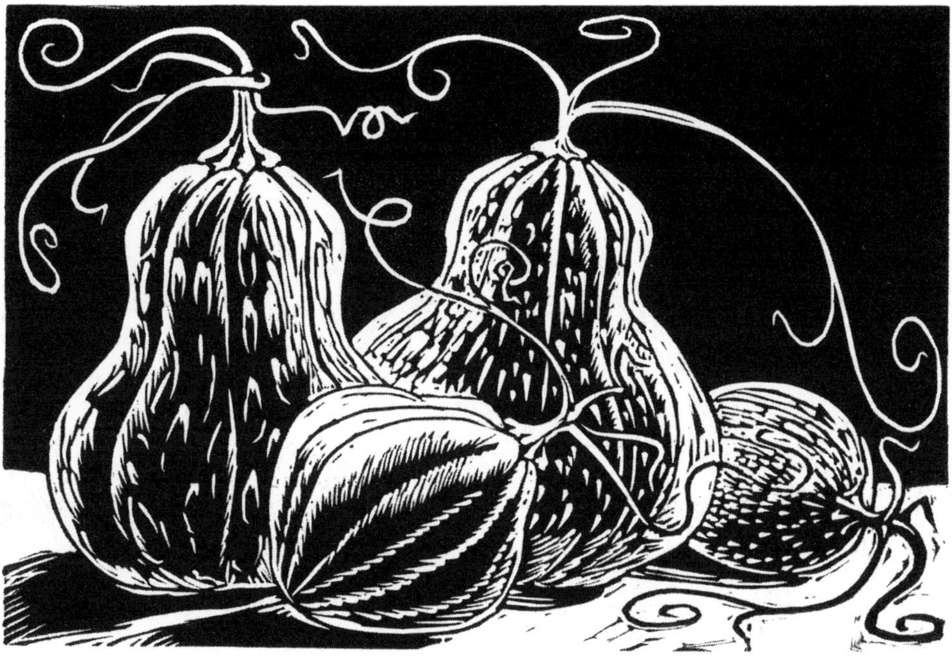

22 Gourds and Squash

We left these to ramble over the compost heap and were rewarded with many examples in different forms and colours at the start of the autumn.

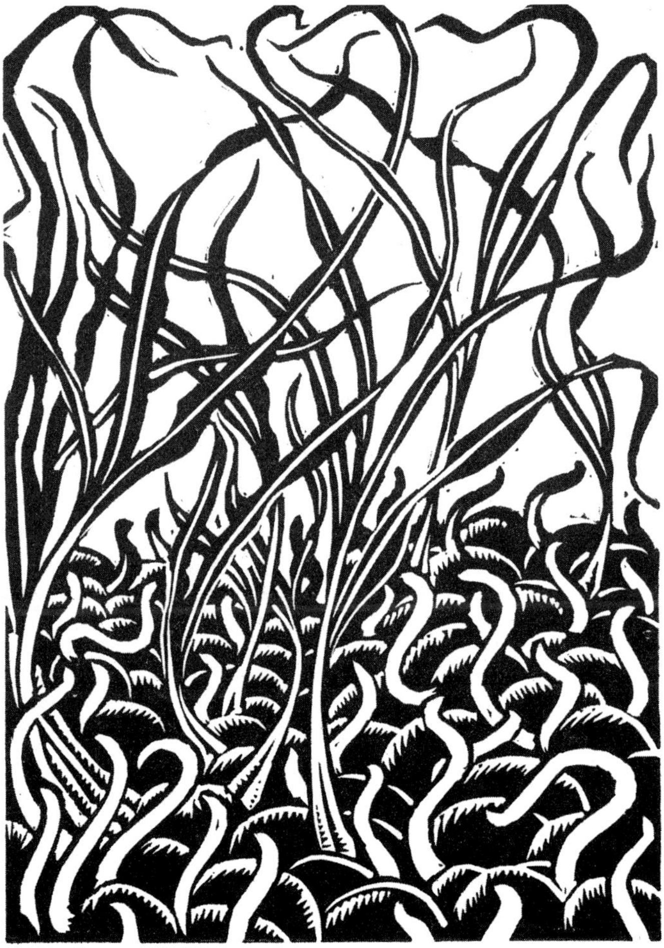

23 Sprouting Birdseed

I was given this in a plastic container to stick to the outside of the kitchen window. The birds completely ignored it and, after a shower of rain, it all began to sprout. I enjoyed trying to draw and engrave the resulting weird and tangled mess.

(I once found Gran, thrilled by the strange plants which had grown in her garden from the seed she'd thrown out from her budgerigar's cage. It turned out to be cannabis: a large, vigorous clump of it!)

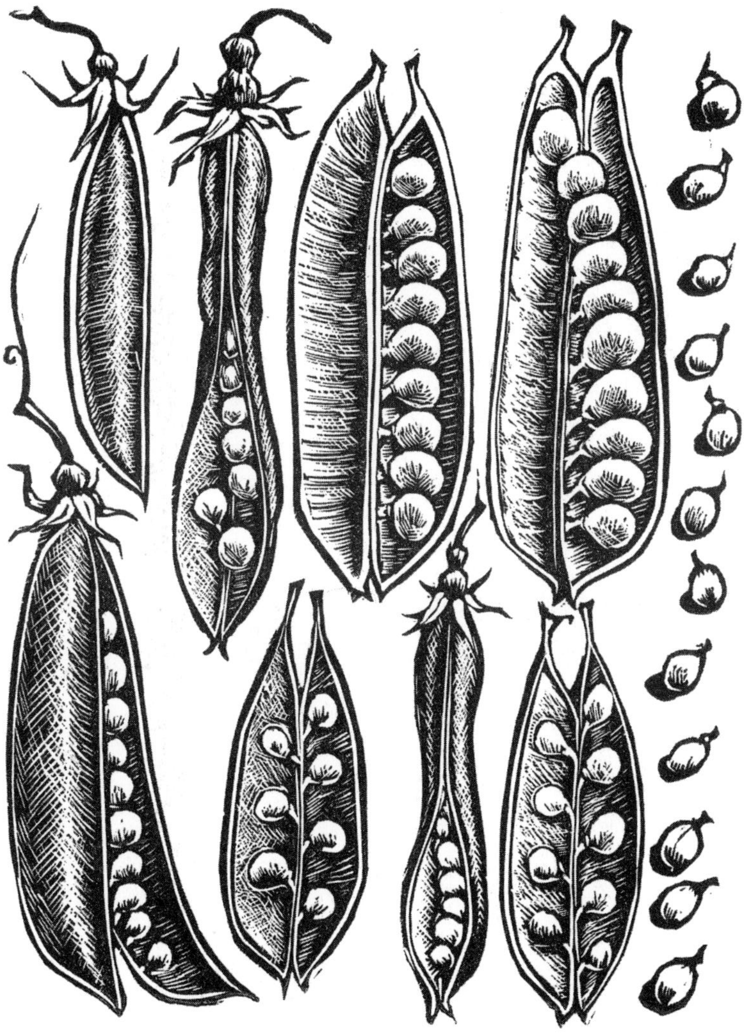

24 Peas

These were like pieces of jewellery laid out on the kitchen table.

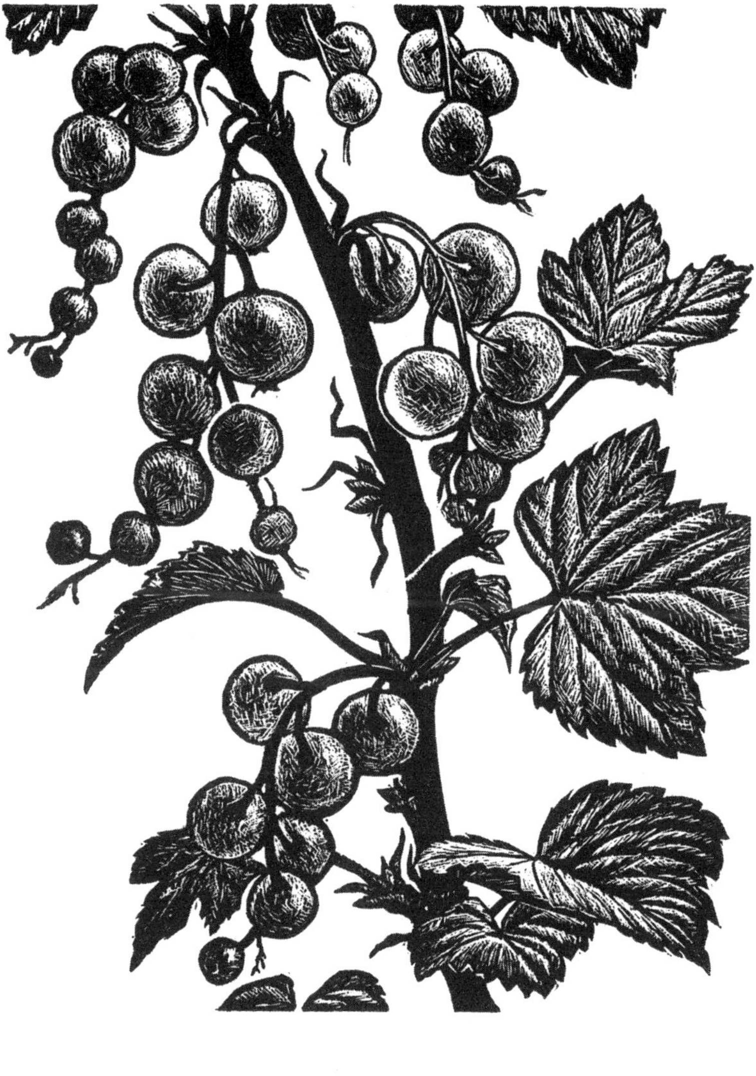

25 Blackcurrants

More 'jewellery' from the allotment.

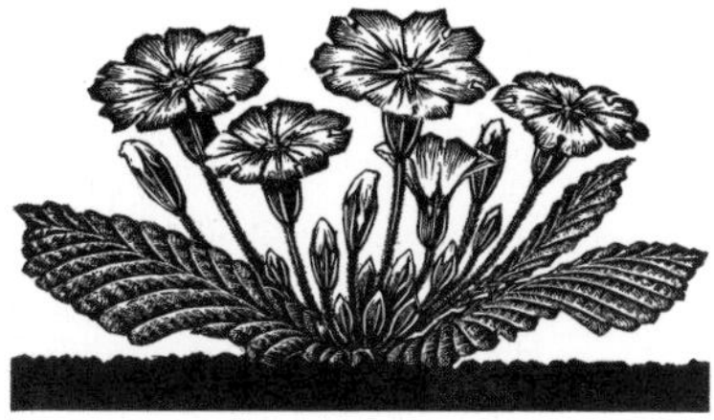

From the Garden

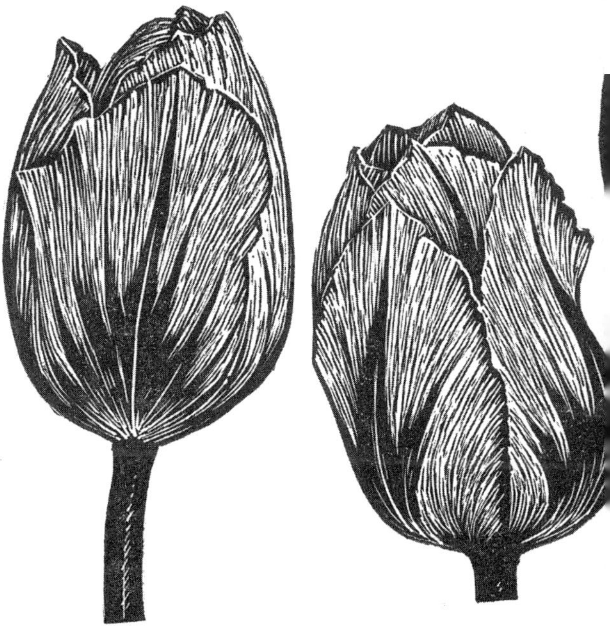

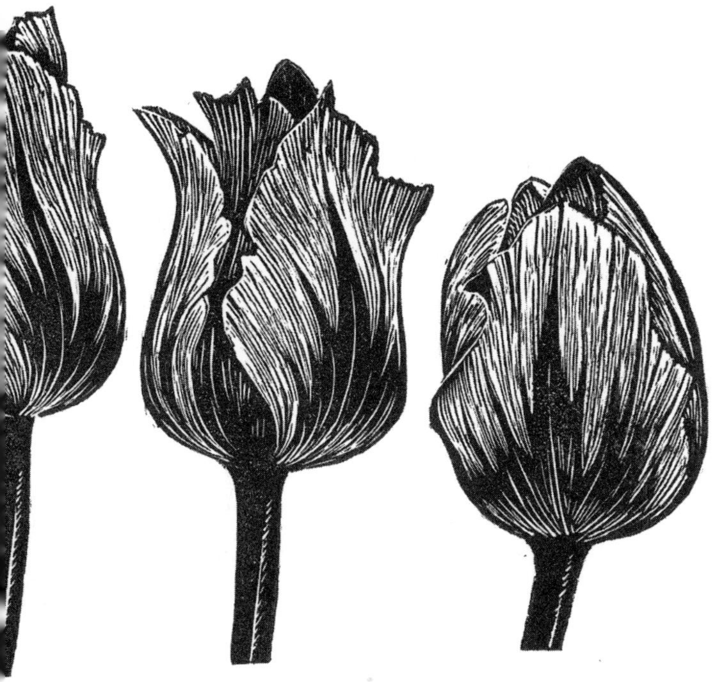

26 Tulips

These specimens combined a wonderful simplicity of form with flame-like markings on the petals and each bloom was subtly different from its neighbour.

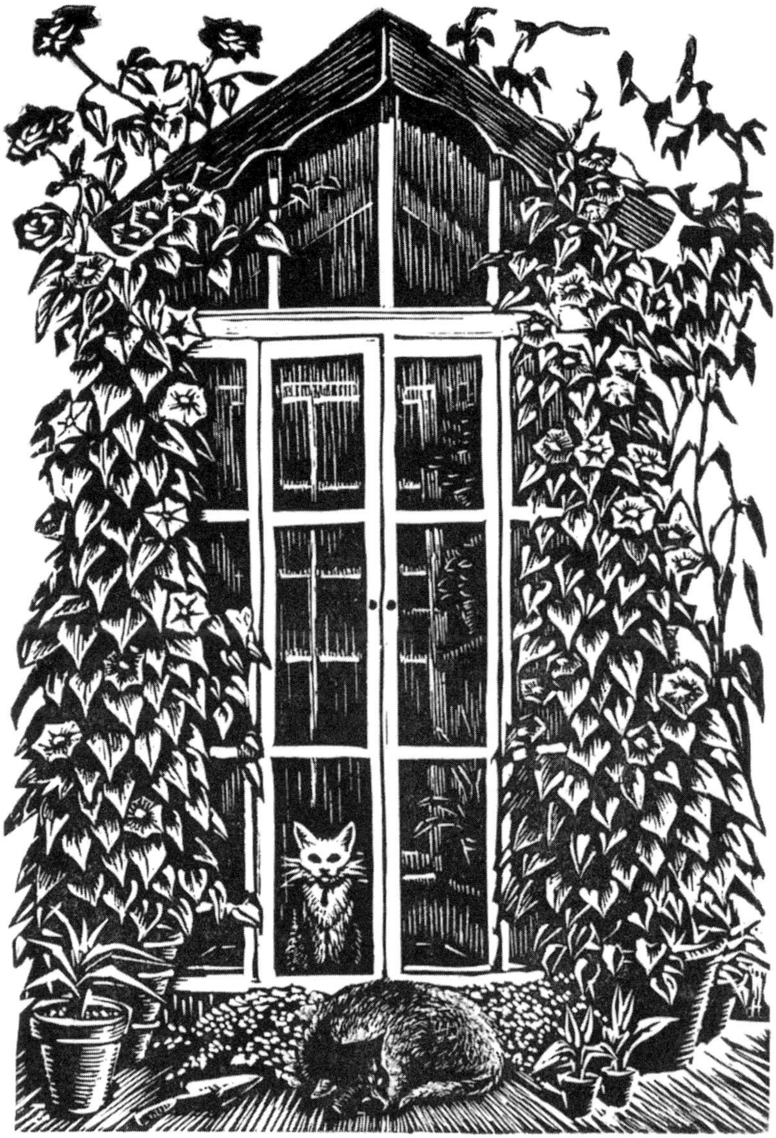

27 Morning Glory (The Porch)

We usually manage to get this beautiful flower to clamber round the porch and I've drawn, painted and engraved it many times over the years.

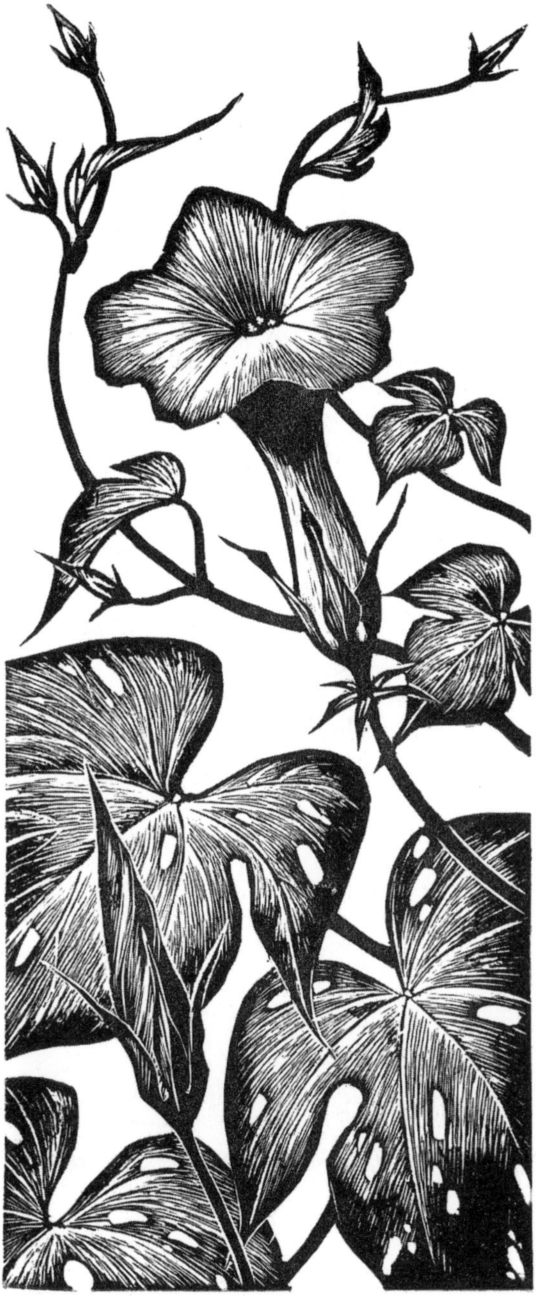

28 Morning Glory Flowers

A very 'Japanese' study.

29 Aquilegia

I prefer the simplest, single-coloured varieties of this plant. These are like delicate, wrought-iron tracery.

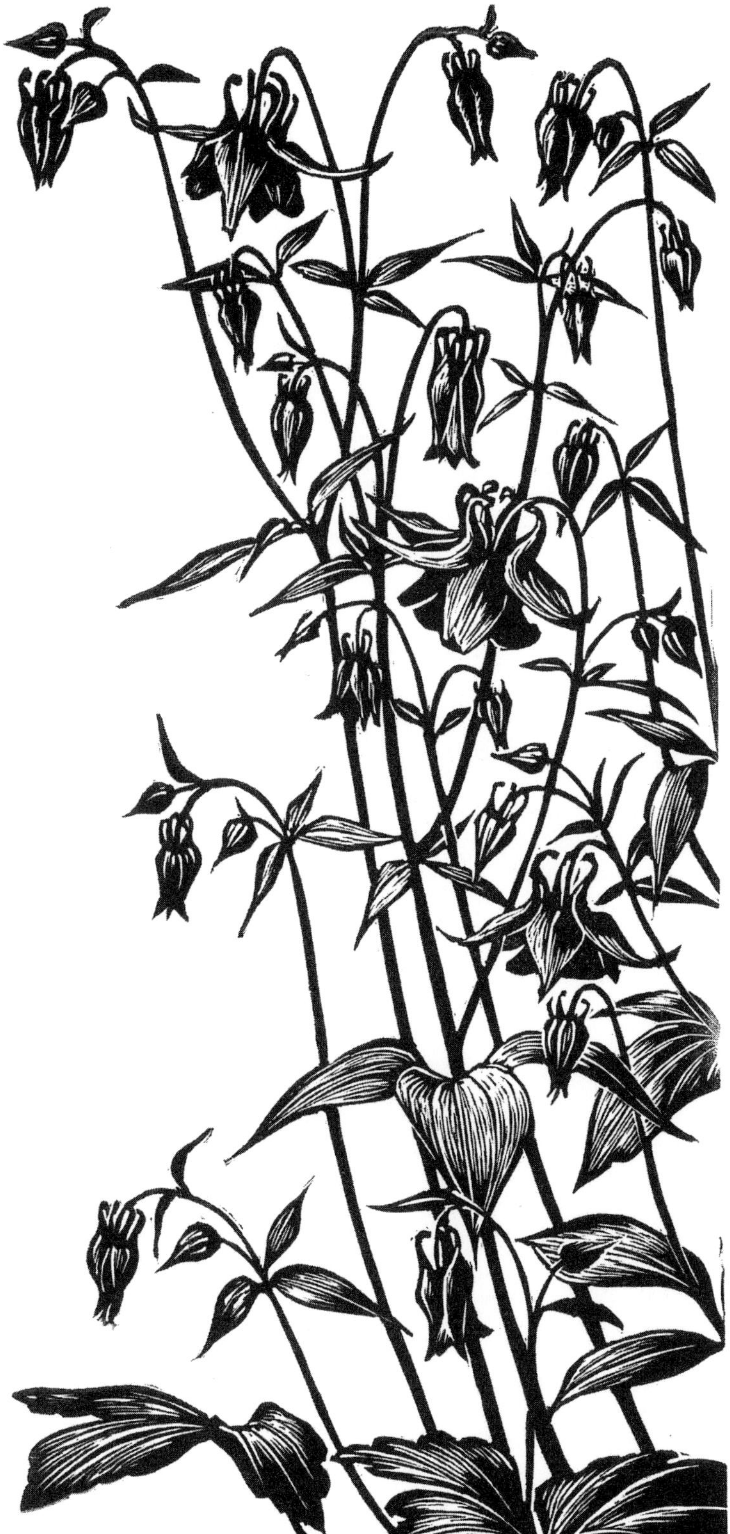

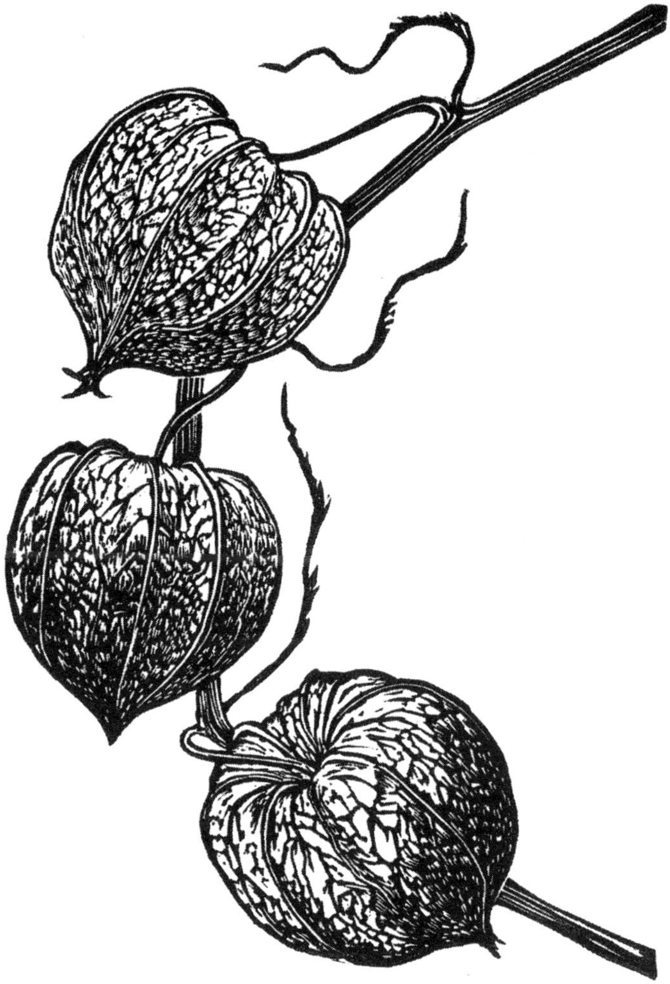

30 Physalis (Japanese Lanterns)

These are a staple art-room visual aid. Many of my pupils must have drawn this specimen. These were the purely decorative kind, not the edible sort known as Cape Gooseberries.

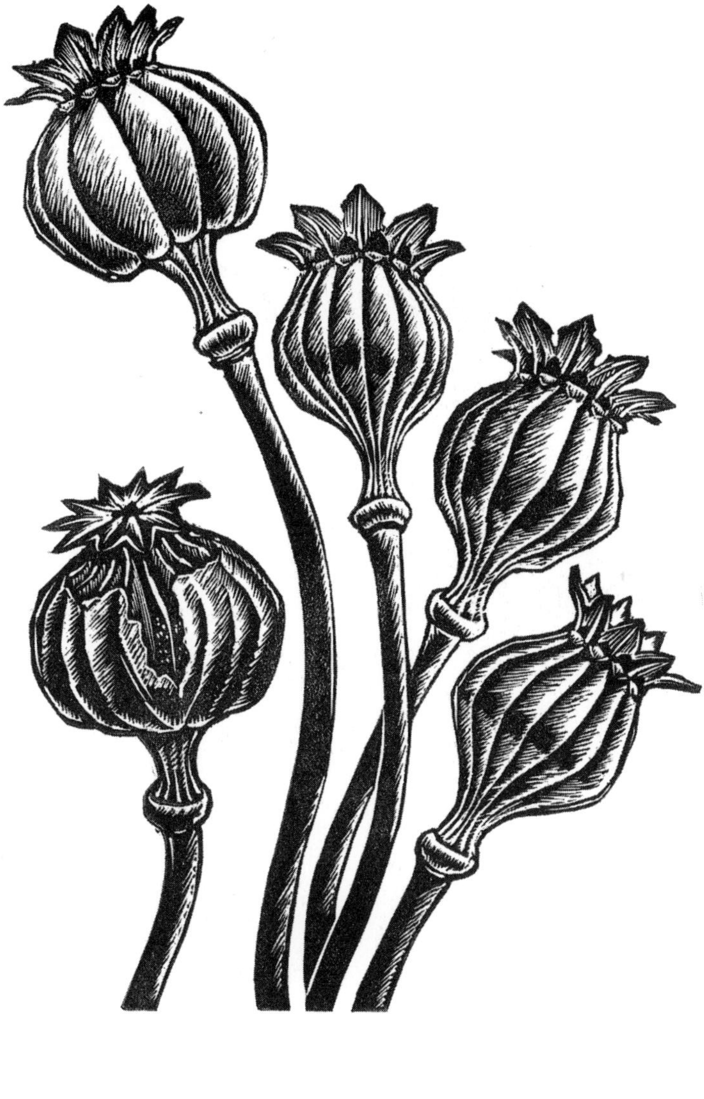

31 Poppy Seedheads

Another staple art-room visual aid.

This was one of the first engravings of a natural form which I attempted.

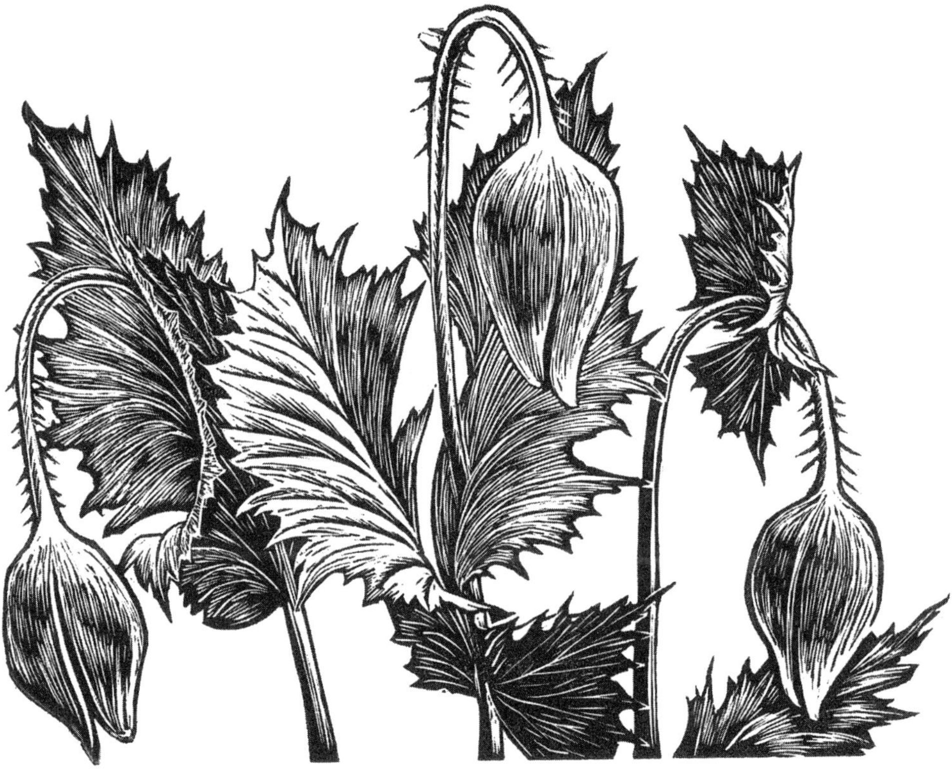

32 Poppies in Bud

Sketched in a friend's garden on the back of an envelope just before they opened up.

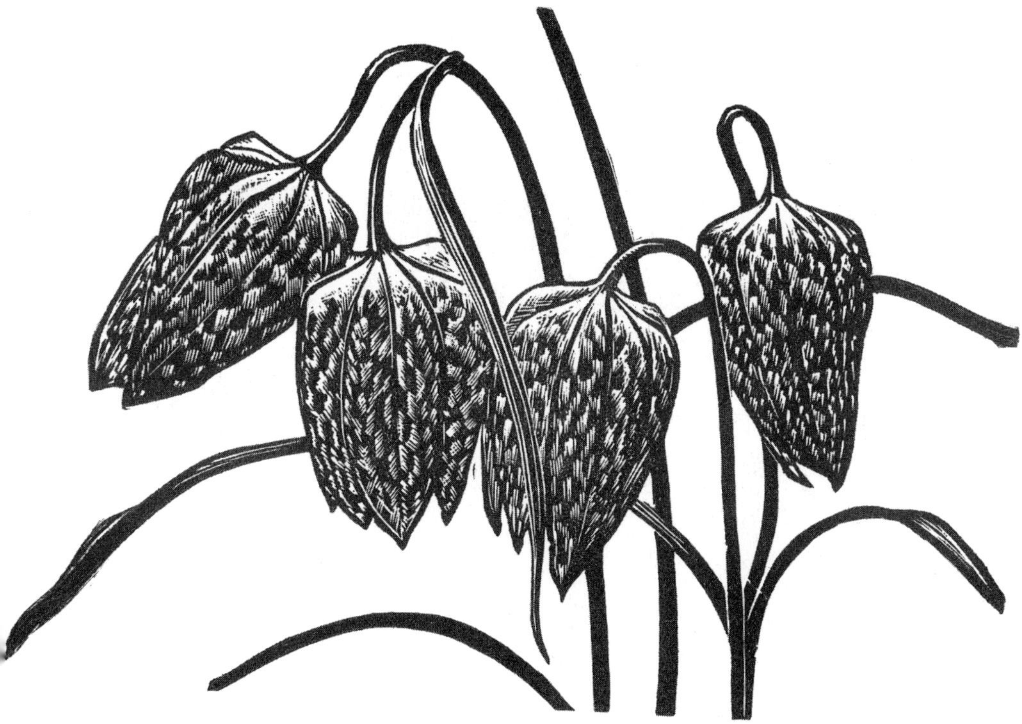

33 Snakeshead Fritillery

These strange and delightful flowers with startling, geometric chequer-board designs on each petal were growing in abundance in a garden which we visited one year. I drew this clump while we were there, and couldn't wait to attempt to grow them in our own garden.

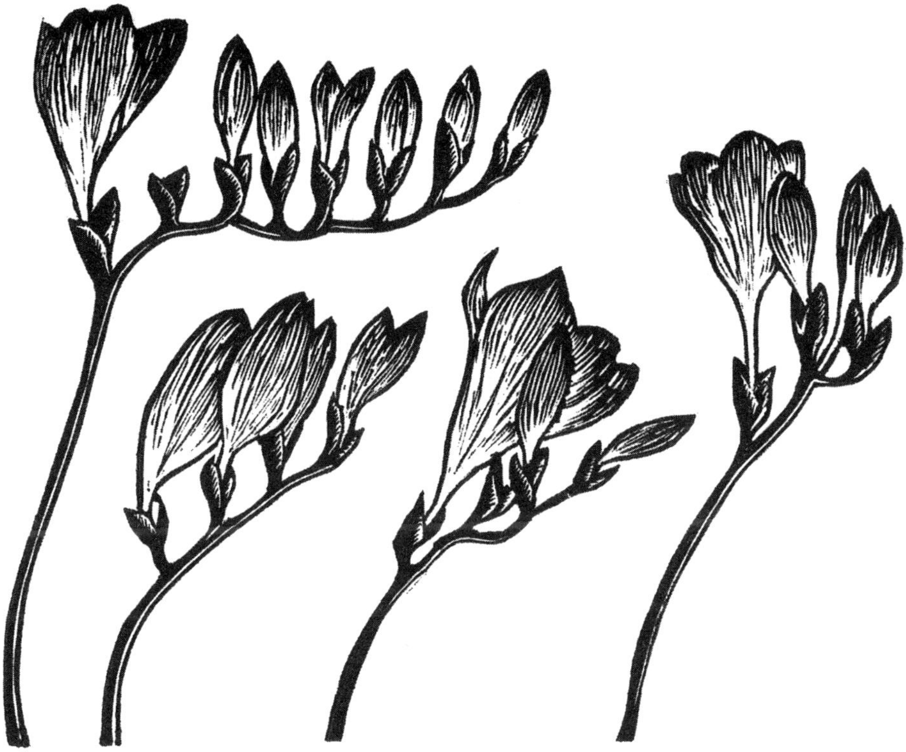

34 Fresia Blooms

A plant where each stem displays, in a most elegant way, the development from bud to open flower.

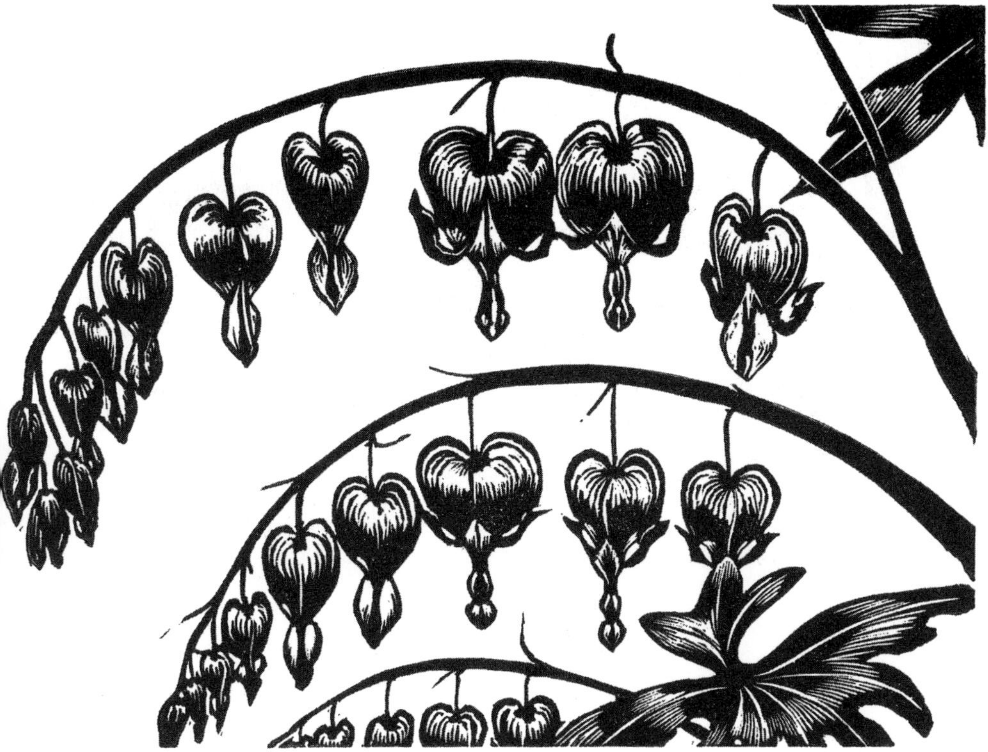

35 Dicentra (The Bleeding Heart Plant)

I remember, as a child, being fascinated by a simpler version of this which grew in my Gran's garden in Yorkshire. It is another plant where each stalk sets out the full development of the flower from bud onwards.

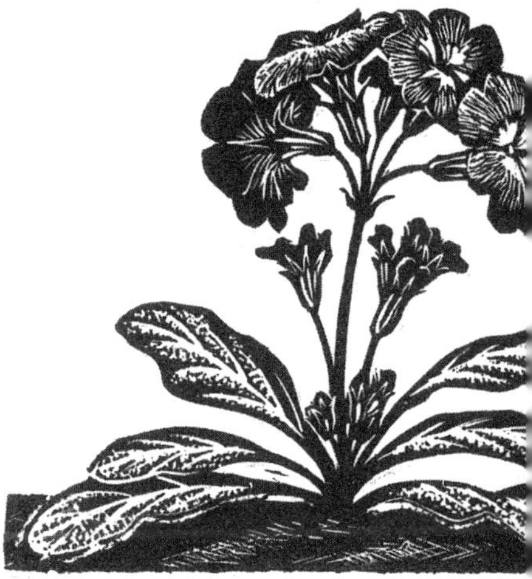

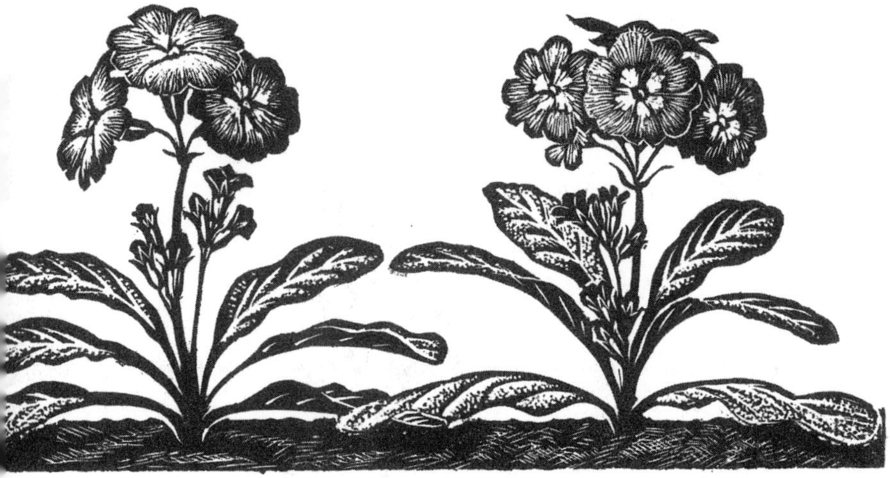

36 Polyanthus

These were growing in a window-box outside the kitchen window so drawing them was a good excuse for not doing the washing up.

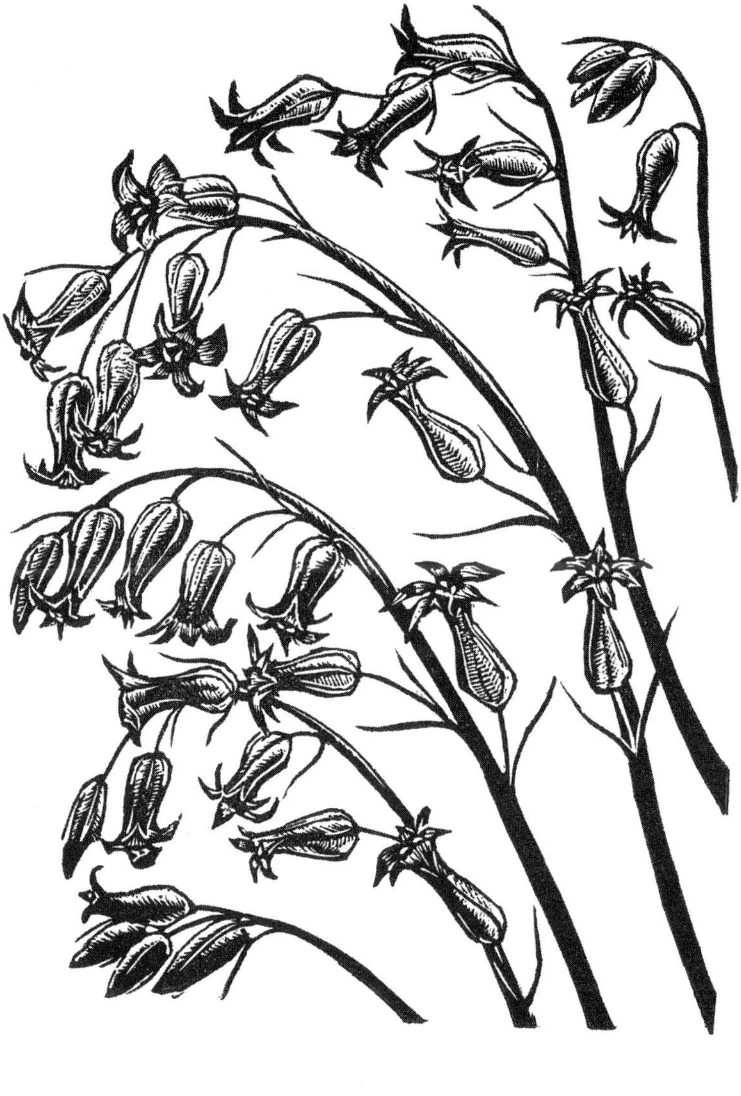

37 Wild Bluebells

These were found in a country lane and the flowers were almost black when in bud. They turned deepest purple as they opened out and were strongly scented.

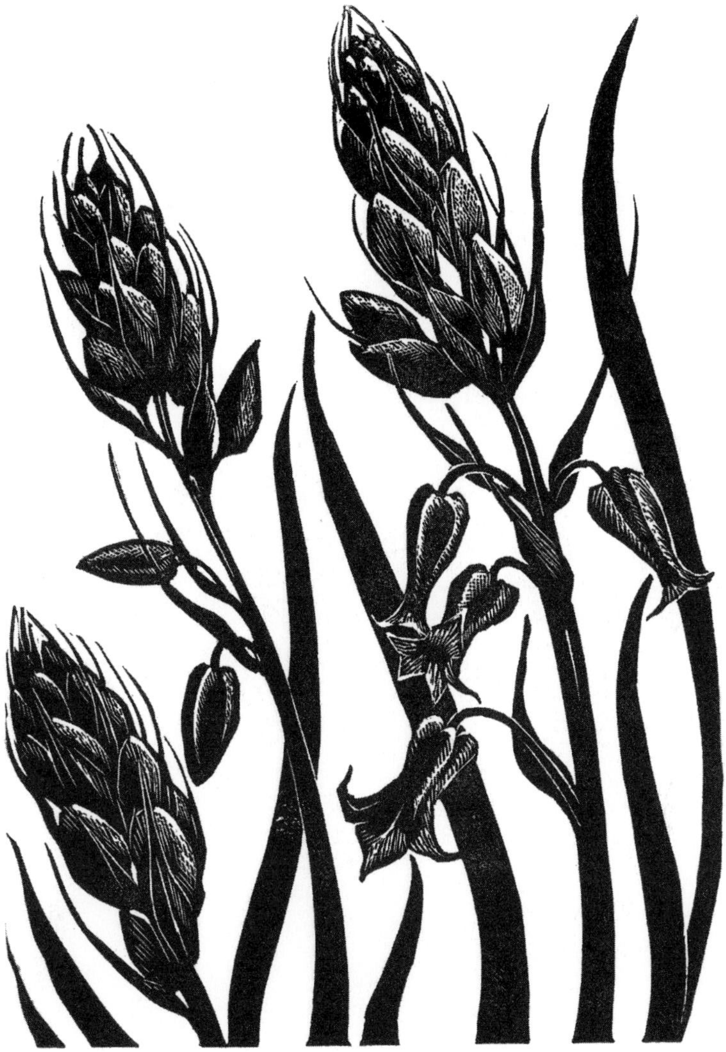

38 Garden Bluebells

These have a tighter form than the wild ones but their colour is rather insipid and they have little perfume. I do like the seedheads which develop from these, though.

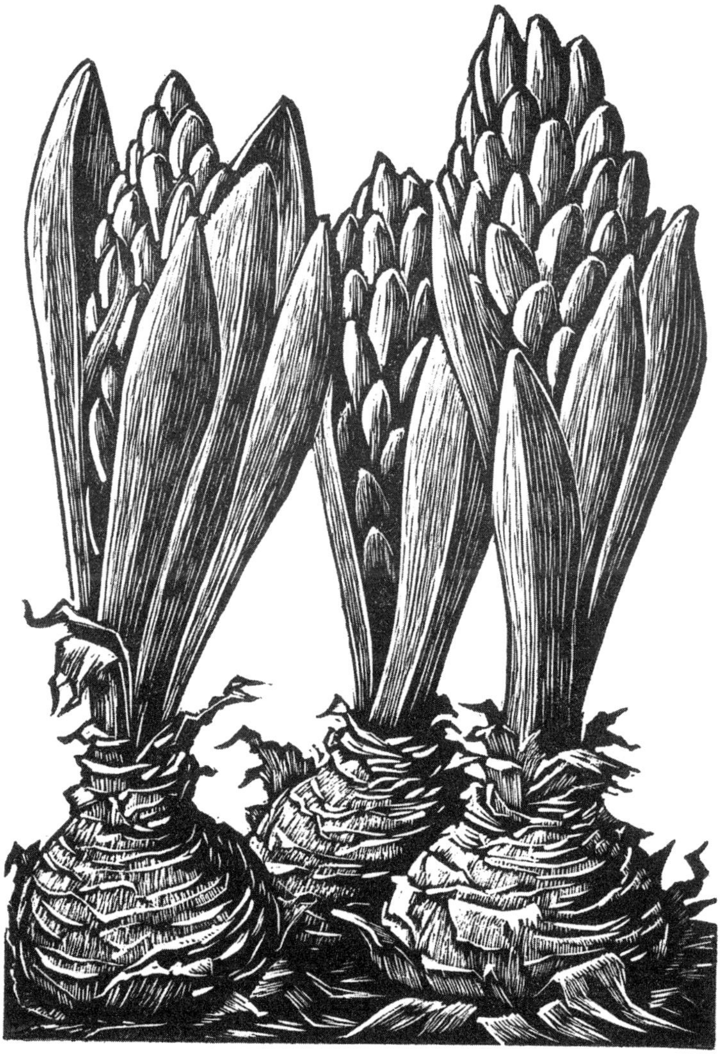

39 Hyacinths

As a child, I remember being shown how to grow one of these bulbs in a glass container by my Great Grandma. I thought it was a magic trick of the first order when it actually began to grow.

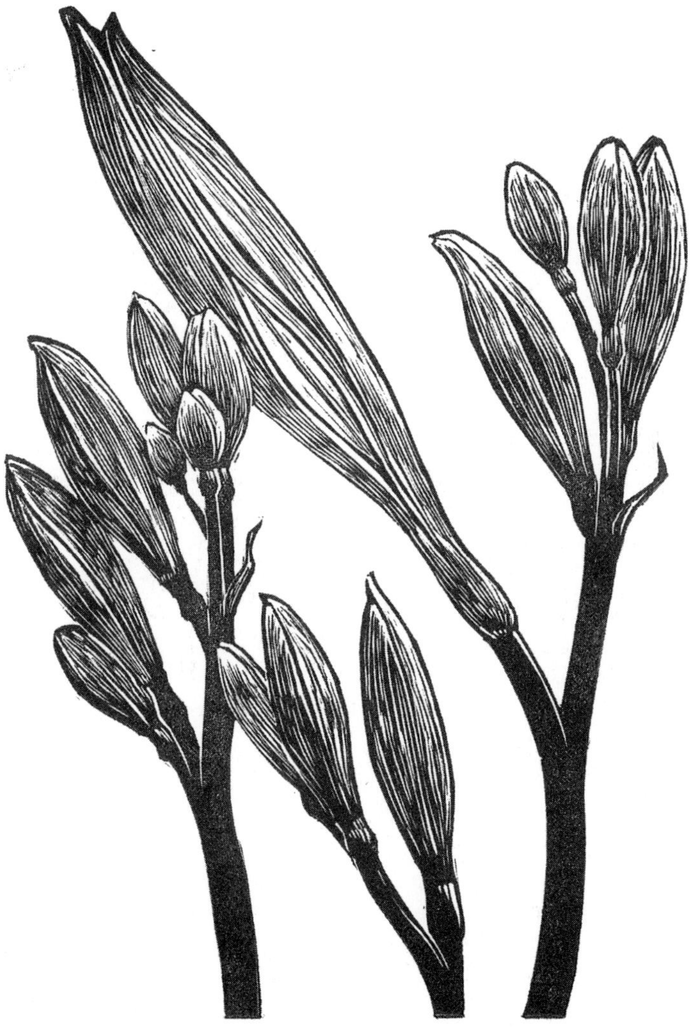

40 Day Lily

Another plant which I drew over a number of days, though I preferred this example in its bud stage.

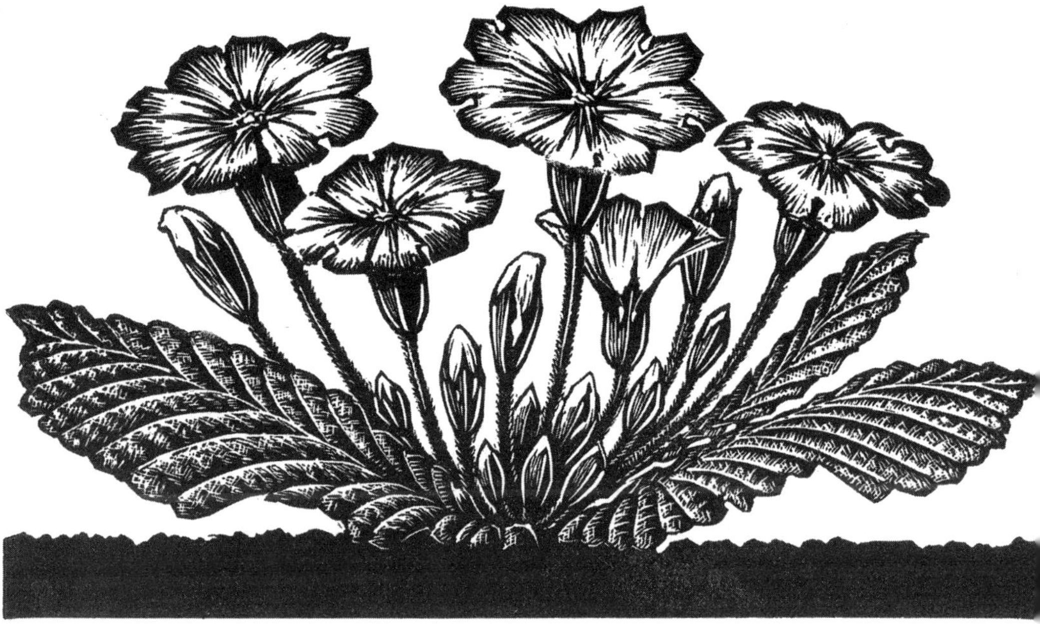

41 Primrose

This engraving was done as a commission for the owner of a certain Primrose Cottage.

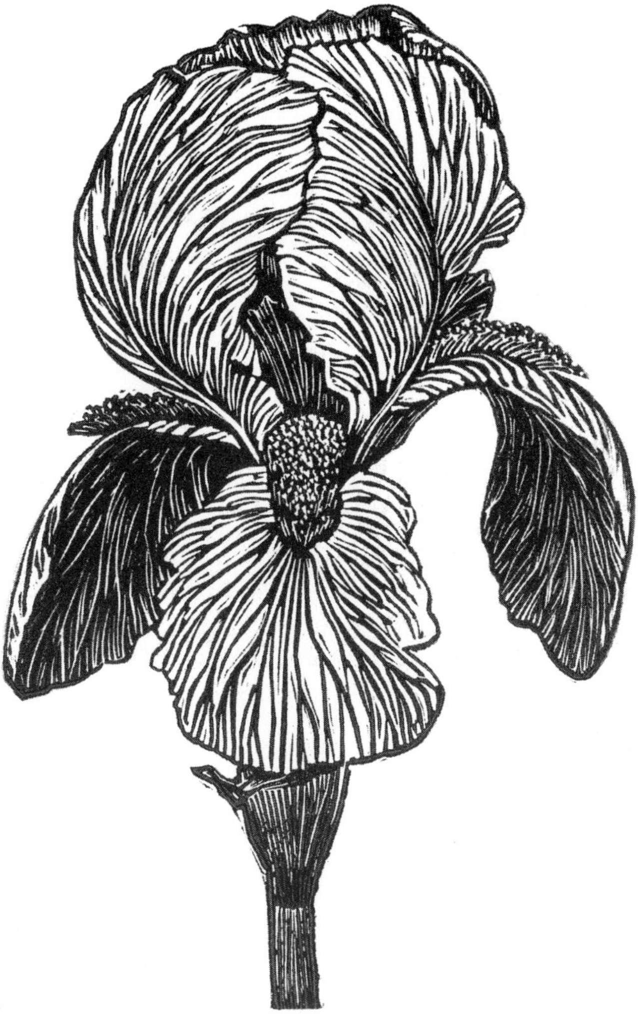

42 Flag Iris

We have quite a collection of these spectacular plants, now, and can't resist adding more each year.

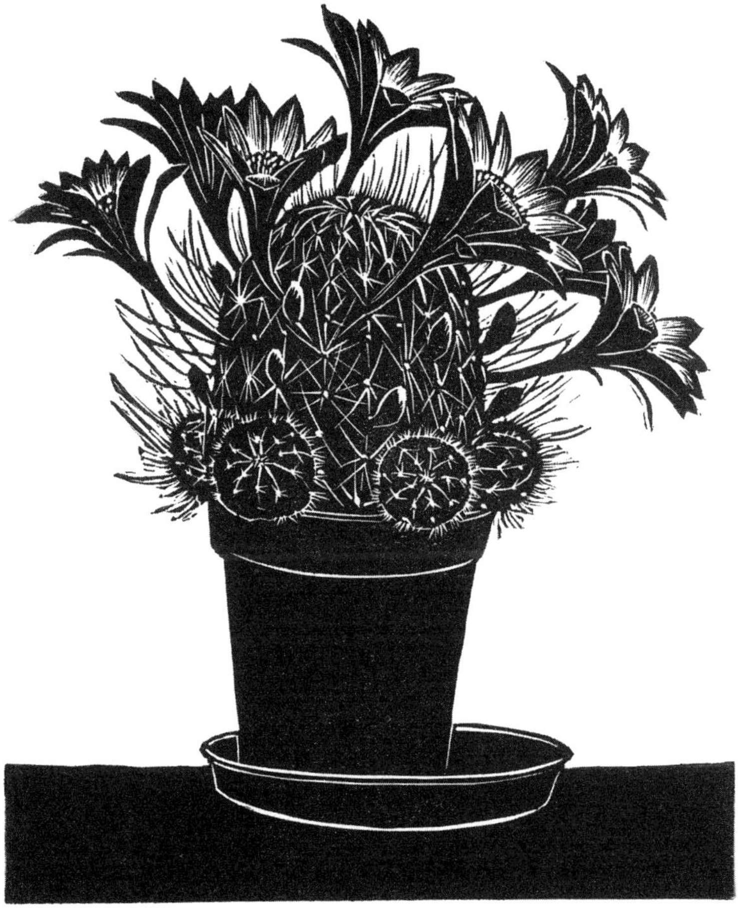

43 Cactus Flowers

I kept a collection of cactus plants on a windowsill of the art-room in the school where I taught and many of my pupils made drawings from them.

This one was always covered in blooms each year. I liked the contrast between the strong, aggressive form of the plant itself and the delicacy of the flowers.

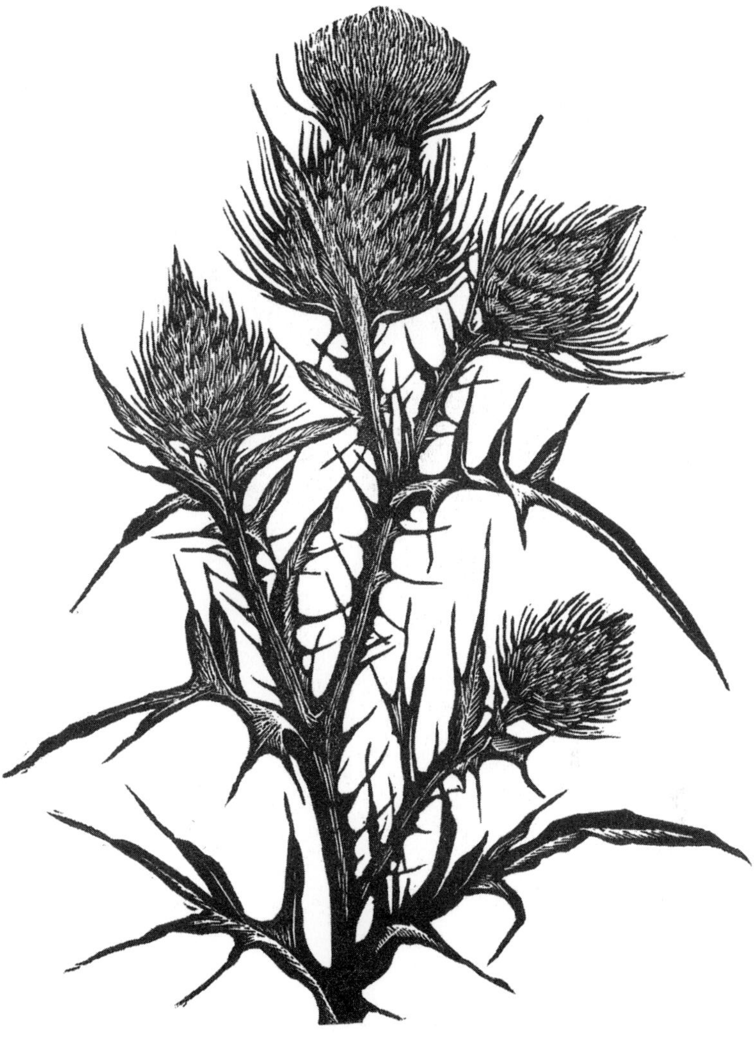

44 Thistle Flowers

Sketched, growing in amongst the six-foot high weeds on the untended allotment plot next to ours when we first took it on. The present owner of the plot would certainly not tolerate such an unwelcome invader.

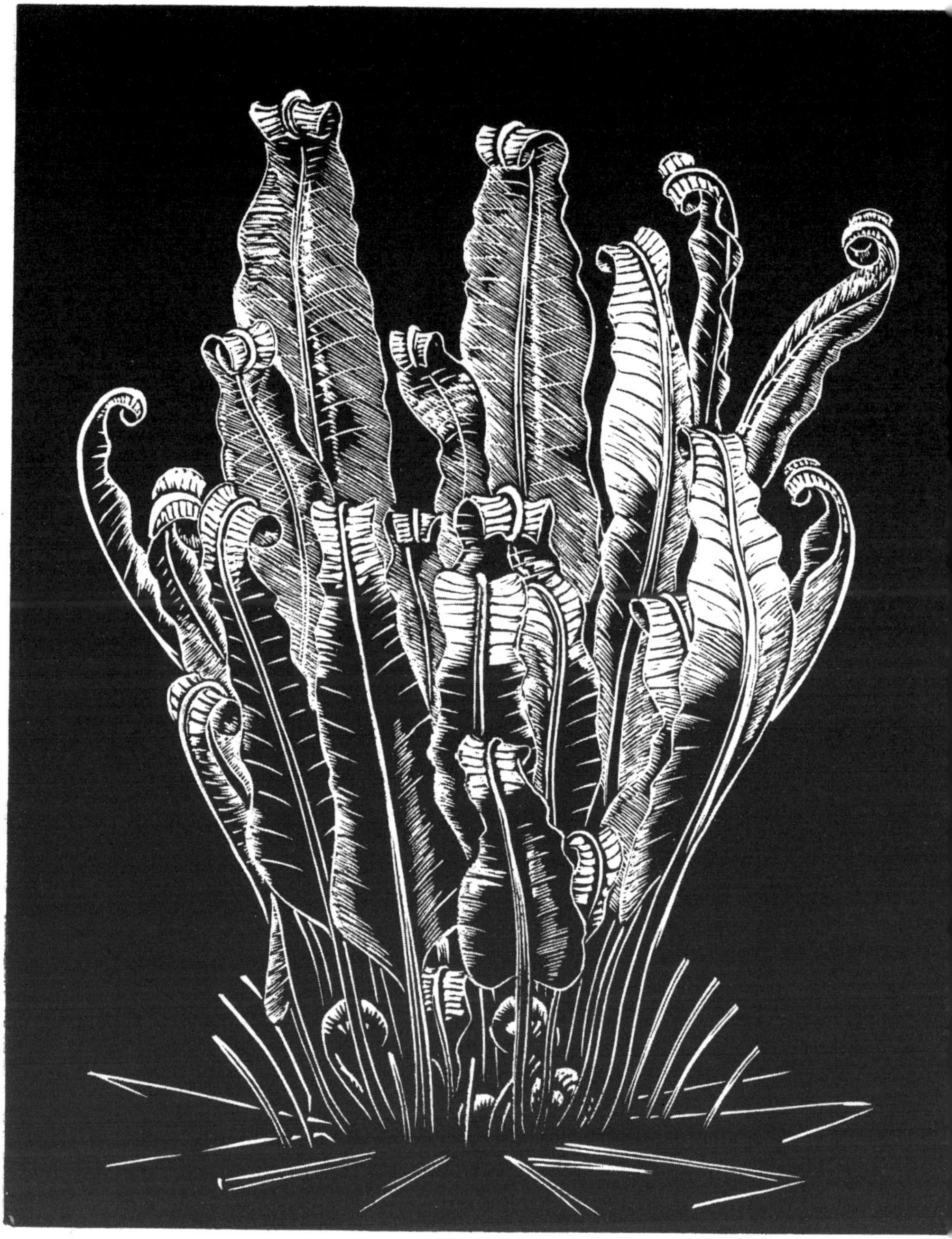

45 Lamb's Tongue Fern

(Reduced from c. 20.5mm x 17.5mm, 8 x 7 inches)

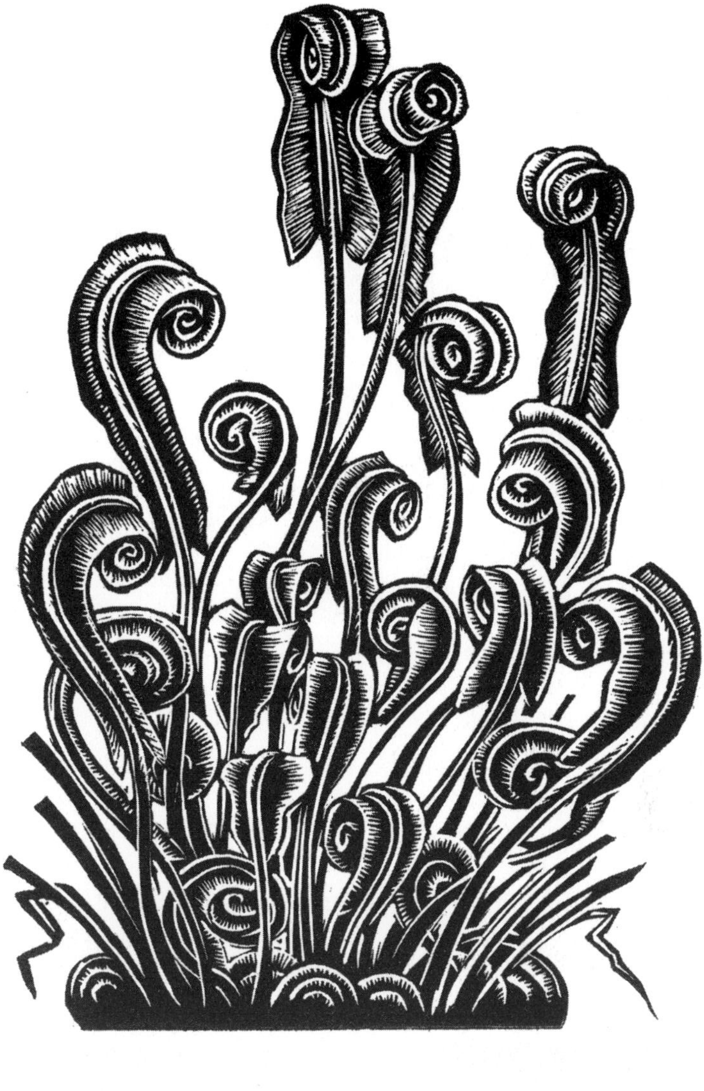

46 Sprouting Ferns

When these start unfurling around the garden you really do feel they should be accompanied by the sound of fireworks going off.

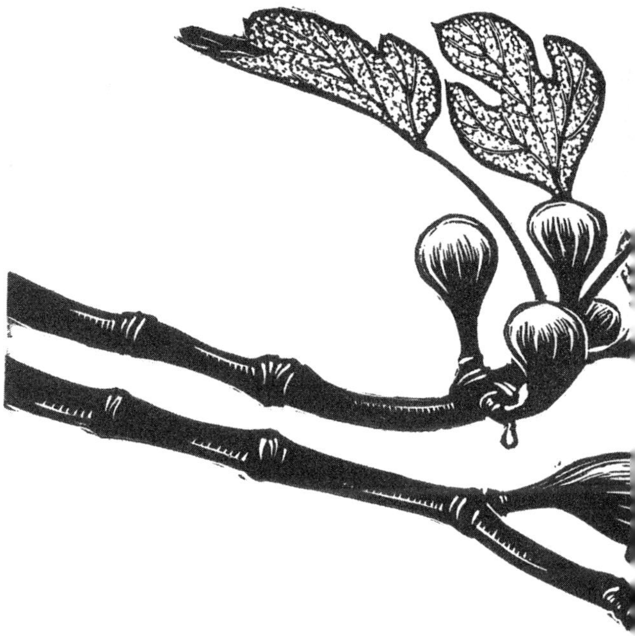

47 Fig Tree

This overhangs the kitchen window. I drew it just after a shower of rain.

The rhythms of the branches and leaves against the sky reminded me of some of the prints by the Japanese masters whom I admire, such as Hokusai and Hiroshige.

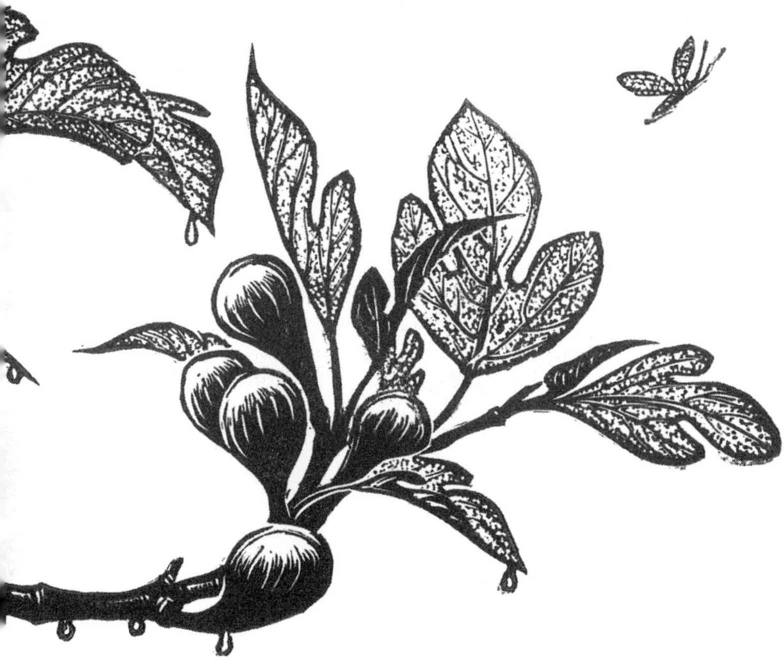

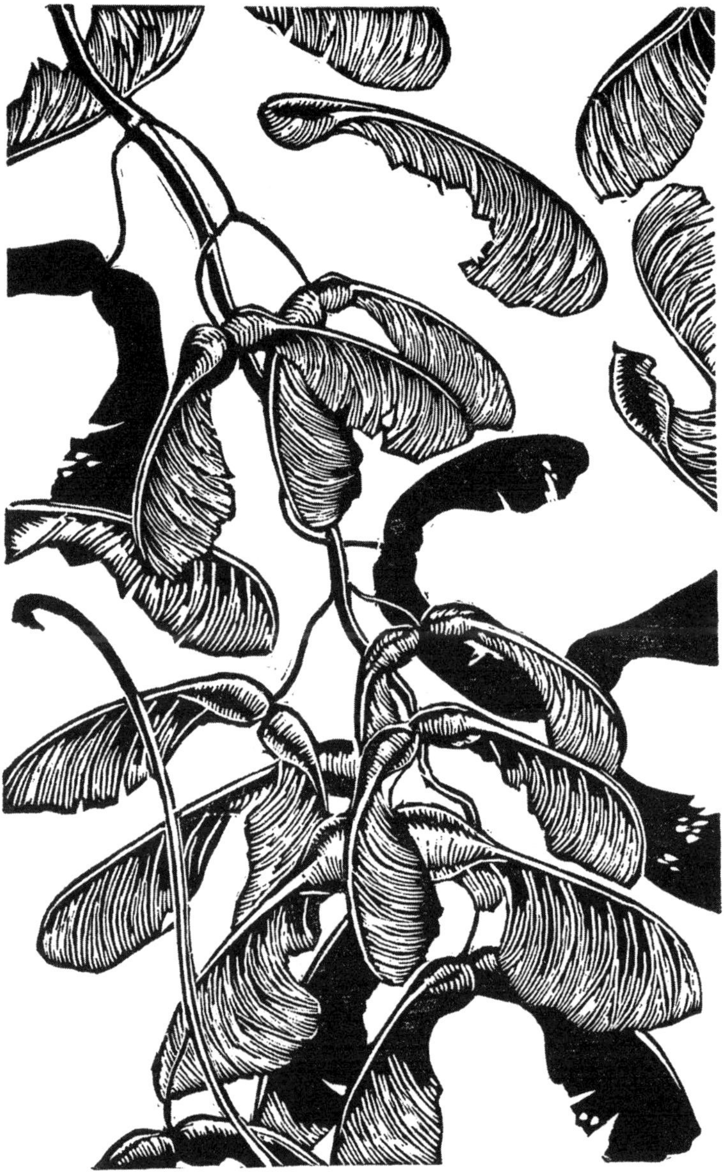

48 Sycamore Seeds

We soon learned to beware of allowing even a single one of these to take root in the garden but they are a pleasure to draw.

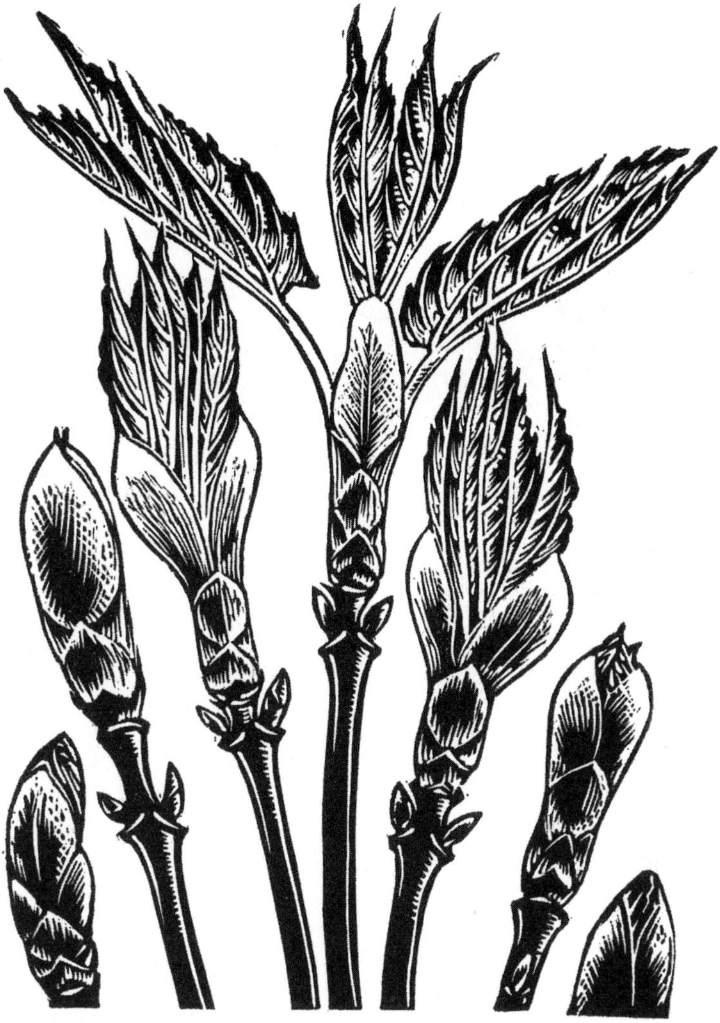

49 Sycamore Buds

The same shoot sketched over a number of days. The young leaves were a beautiful bronze colour when they began to open out.

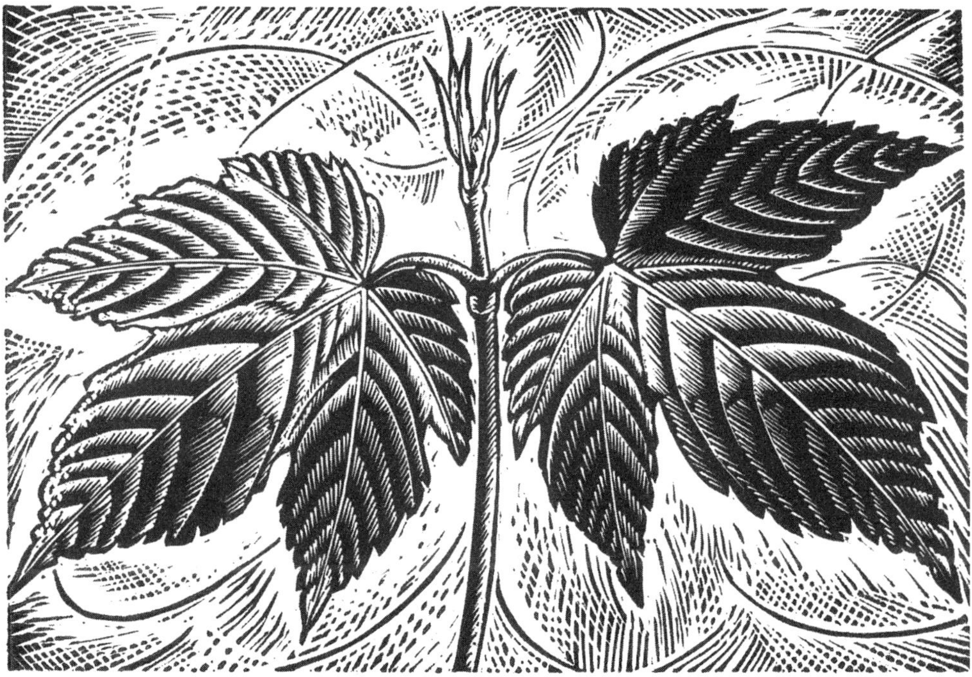

50 Two Sycamore Leaves

Another attempt to learn to love a tree which has been a bit of a scourge in our garden over the years.

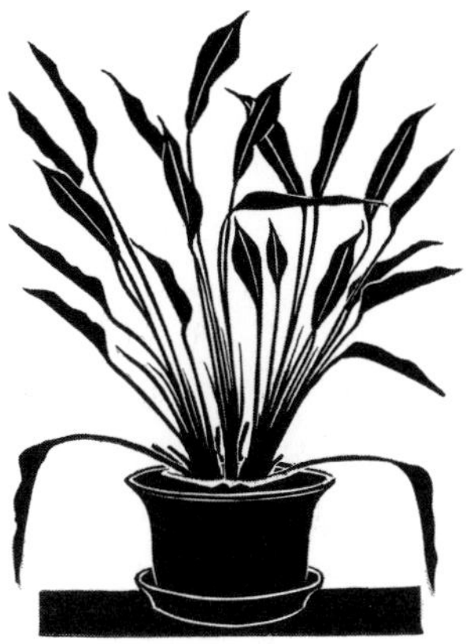

From the House

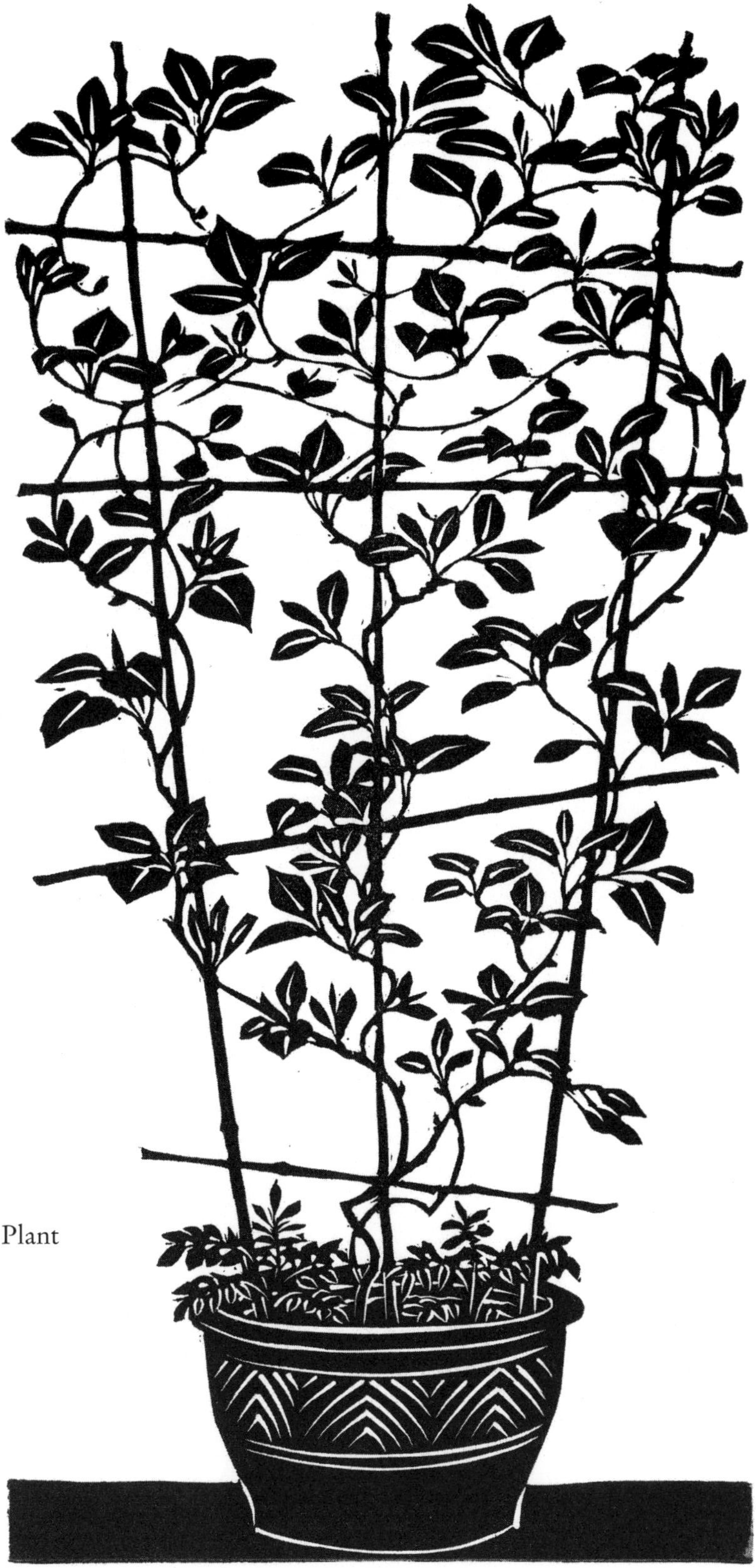

51 Pot Plant

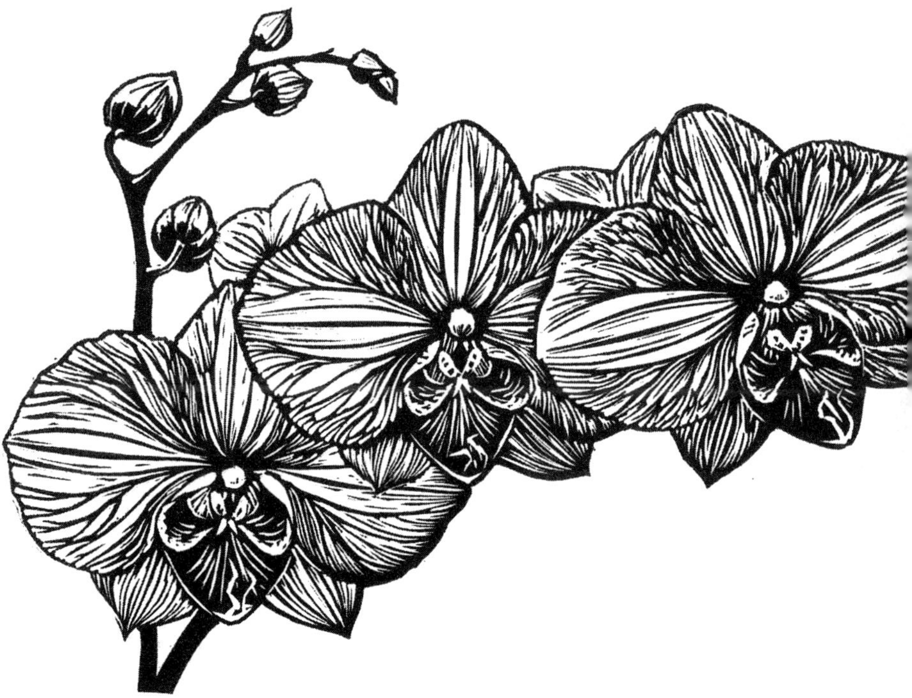

52 Moth Orchid

I went through a phase of collecting these exotic plants. The flowers last for a long time and develop slowly, so I enjoyed drawing the forms of each bloom and the veined designs on the petals of this example.

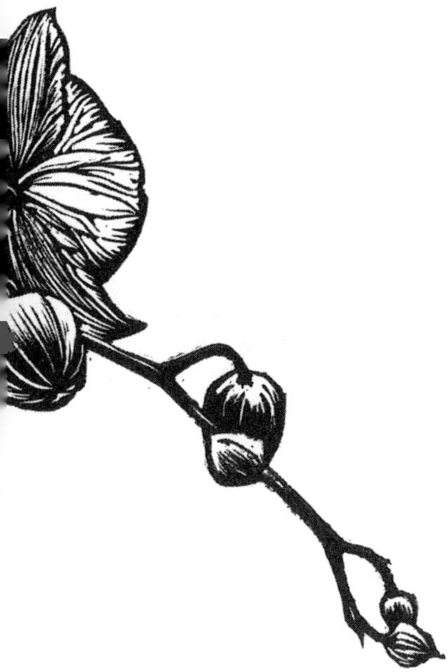

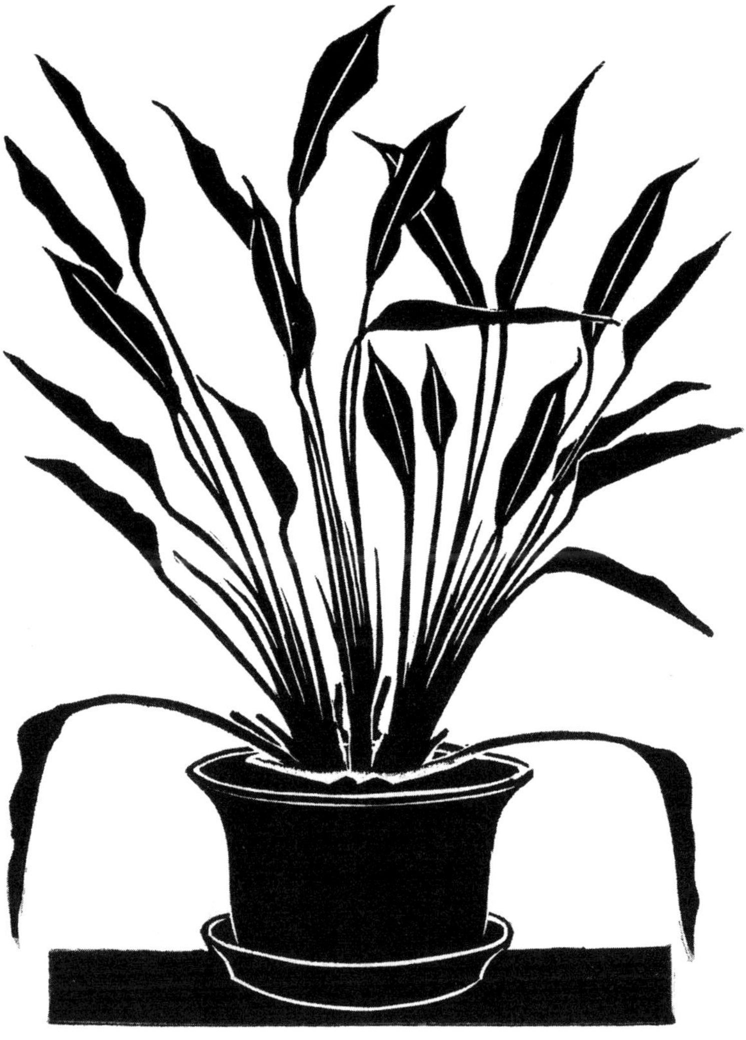

53 Foliage Houseplants

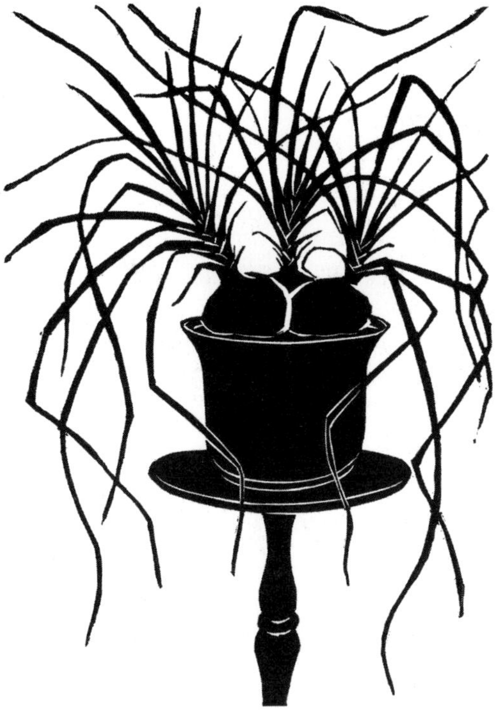

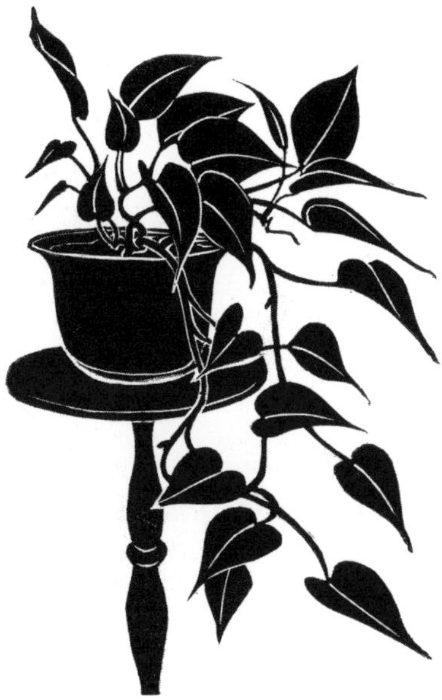

54 and 55 (Reduced from c. 140mm x 95mm c. 5 1/2 x 3 3/4 inches)

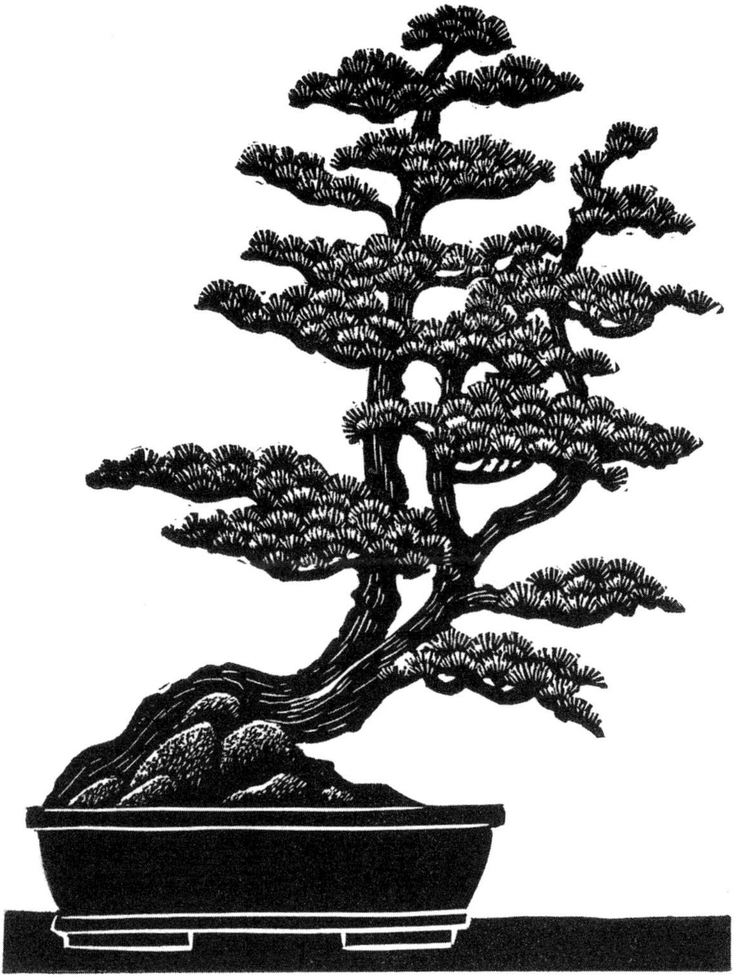

56 Bonsai Trees

My own attempts at tending these plants only left me with more admiration than ever for those people who are truly skilful at this art.

When it is well-done, the miniaturisation can be breathtakingly beautiful.

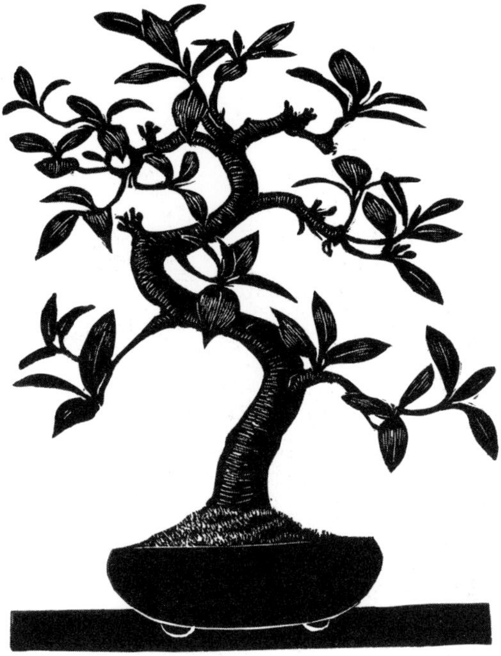

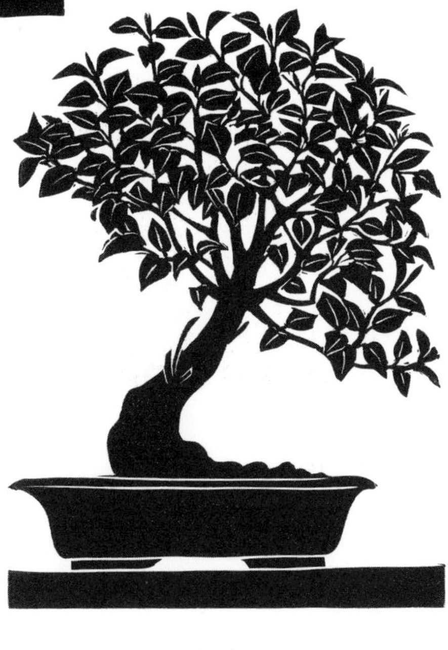

57 and 58 (Reduced from c. 140mm x 95mm, c. 5 1/2 x 3 3/4 inches)

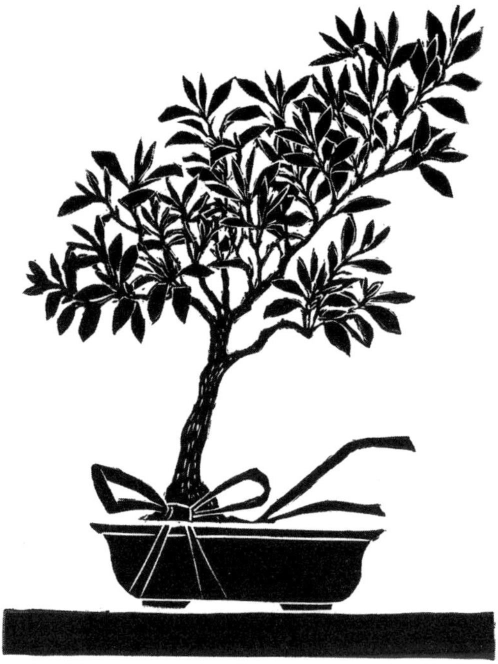

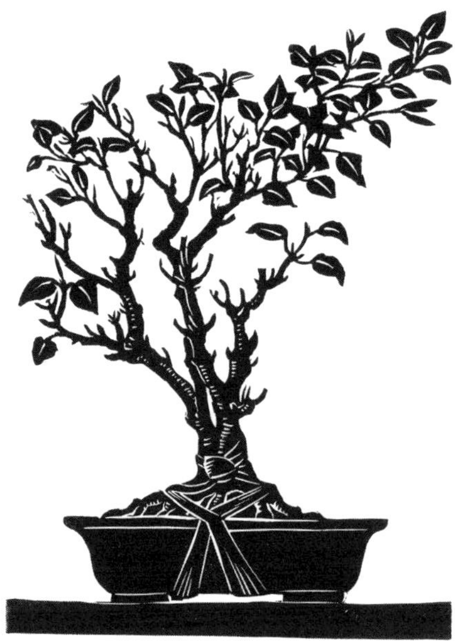

59 and 60 (Reduced from c. 140mm x 95mm, c. 5 1/2 x 3 3/4 inches)

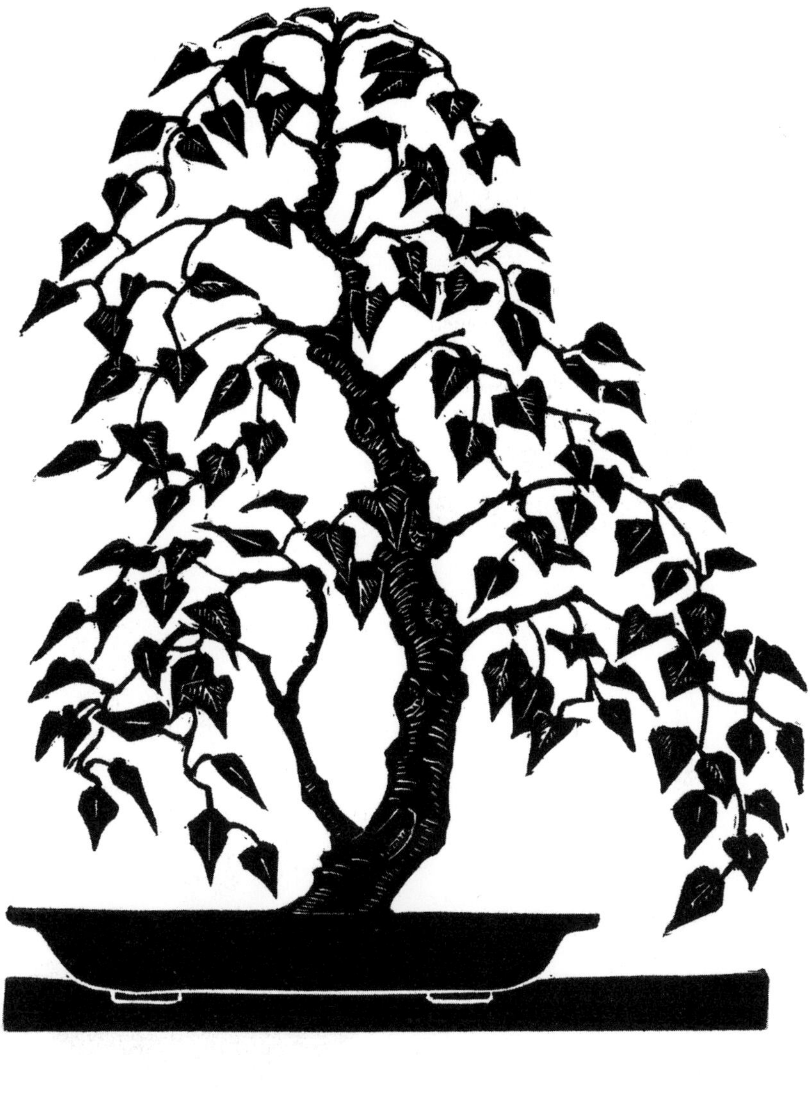

61

About the Artist

Trevor Haddrell was born in Rotherham, South Yorkshire and moved south to train as an Art & Design teacher at Bath Academy of Art, Corsham, when Clifford Ellis was the principal there. He later completed a BA Hons degree through the Open University. He taught at Ashton Park School, Bristol from 1967, eventually becoming head of department. He then moved to Clifton High School as Head of Art & Design in 1984, and retired from teaching in 2000.

Over the years, Trevor Haddrell has had many shared and one-man shows of paintings, drawings and relief prints at a number of local venues. He has exhibited several times in the three-yearly National Print shows at the Royal West of England Academy, winning a prize for a panoramic print of Bristol Docks in 1997. He also exhibits regularly with the Society of Wood Engravers. His work is in many private collections, in Bristol Museum & Art Gallery and the Theatre Collection of Bristol University.

His acclaimed **Panoramic Bristol** was published by Redcliffe Press in 2002.

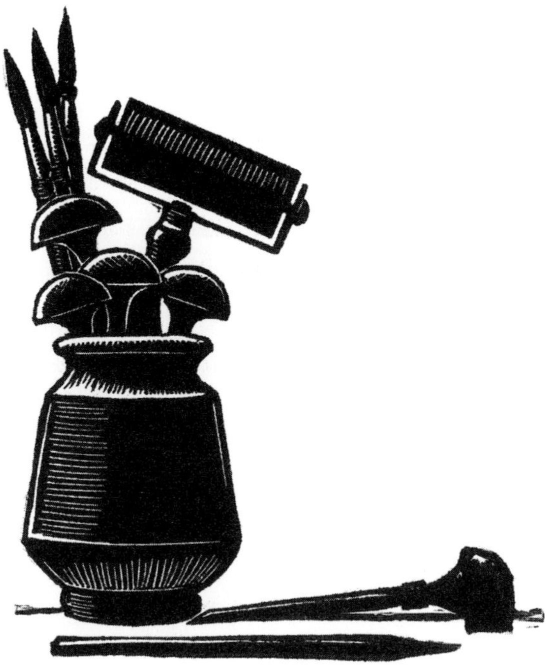

With many thanks to all those who have been so encouraging and supportive over the years.

Trevor Haddrell
Woodwell Cottage
October 2005

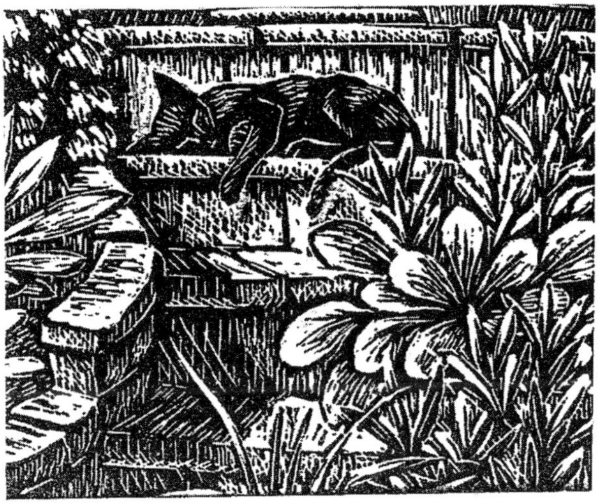

Tel: 0117 929 8363